ACQUIRING MORE PROFIT

THE DEFINITIVE GUIDE TO SUCCESSFUL REAL
ESTATE BROKERAGE MERGERS & ACQUISITIONS

BY
GEORGE SLUSSER
VICTOR LUND

Copyright © 2023 by George Slusser & Victor Lund
Paperback 979-8-9880388-1-8

Library of Congress Control Number 2023905674

All rights reserved. No part of this publication may be reproduced or transmitted in any form or by any means, electronic or mechanical, including photocopying, recording, or by any information storage and retrieval system without written permission of the authors, except where permitted by law.

Published by WAV Group – Arroyo Grande, CA
Printed in the United States of America

Dedications

I would like to dedicate this book to our WAV Group clients. My wife, Marilyn, and I relocated to California after Fisher-Price was sold to Mattel. Marilyn was an executive with Fisher-Price, leading the marketing department, and was elevated to lead the global strategic planning for Mattel globally. After the earn-out was complete, we focused on consulting for venture capital endeavors, and Marilyn became CEO of Surveyor Corporation.

When venture capital collapsed in the late '90s, we focused all of our energy on consulting. Mike Audet joined WAV Group to lead our real estate division in 2001. Little did we know at the time that real estate could become our exclusive focus.

WAV Group started by creating centers of excellence in strategic planning and vendor selection for MLSs. A major innovation we brought to real estate strategic planning was to focus our preparation through broker and agent satisfaction surveys and interviews. We realized that real estate brokers' communications with the MLS were largely broken. On call after call after call, brokers told us about their problems with the MLS, most of which were not really problems at all. The brokers were simply in the dark on how to work with their MLS and leverage their services in the best possible way.

It was not long before large enterprise brokerages and franchises engaged us to help them with their technology strategy — expanding our services beyond MLS and into brokerage.

For the longest time, we avoided the M&A segment of services to brokerages. The team at Real Trends was doing a great job, and we did not believe that we had the experience to deliver a comparable quality of service.

In 2021, George Slusser joined WAV Group after his retirement from decades at Realogy. He brought with him the experience of thousands of valuations and more than 700 closed acquisitions. We then added Finley Hair, with his decades of successful M&A and leadership experience in the industry.

Shortly thereafter, our friend and client Mark McLaughlin traded Pacific Union to Compass in one of the largest transactions in brokerage history. Today, WAV Group has the best M&A team in the real estate industry.

Our MLS, brokerage, and real estate technology clients have enriched our lives with friendships that will last a lifetime. I am forever grateful for each and every one of you.

Victor

I echo Victor's thanks to the real estate industry that has blessed me and our family with so much. I am grateful to the many people at all my stops through the years whom I now call friends.

I am thankful for our wonderful children and grandchildren, who are the joy and inspiration for my life. I am proud of their accomplishments and look forward to them all continuing to blossom and excel as exceptional individuals.

Although I am so very fortunate and thankful for my family and friends, there is only one person with more impact on my life than any other. I dedicate this book, along with my eternal gratitude, to my wife June, who has supported me, guided me, and even pushed me when needed. She is the love of my life, trusted partner, and my best friend.

George

Advance Reviews

A must read: **Acquiring More Profit**, *The Definitive Guide to Successful Real Estate Brokerage Mergers & Acquisitions*; by George Slusser and Victor Lund

2023 and 2024 present new and unique opportunities for real estate brokerage owners. Many brokerage leaders will seek to expand their market share through mergers or acquisitions in these changing times. In virtually every real estate marketplace over the past 40-plus years, our industry has seen top brokerage firms significantly expand their organizations utilizing acquisitions as one of their primary growth strategies. This year, and going forward, not only will this trend continue, depending upon the successful deployment of these strategies by regional leaders, it may significantly impact our industry's landscape.

Acquiring More Profit, *The Definitive Guide to Successful Real Estate Brokerage Mergers & Acquisitions* by George Slusser and Victor Lund is a must-read for every brokerage executive. I believe there will be many new opportunities for broker/owners to explore and evaluate in terms of expanding their firms, and this book helps breakdown and explain the potential, the challenges and how to make it happen for your business.

For many, many years, I have witnessed George Slusser's work as one of residential real estate's most widely respected experts in all areas impacting mergers and acquisitions, as well as Victor Lund's dedication and achievements in helping to advance our industry. I congratulate George and Victor, and highly recommend reading **Acquiring More Profit**.

John Featherston, Founder & CEO

RIS Media

"We are proof that the principles, tools, and systems described in this book work. This book is even more comprehensive than the first one which has been our M&A foundation for years. We have grown exponentially through M&A by engaging George and the WAV Group on our last seven acquisitions. They assist us with all phases of the M&A process from valuation to closing. We would not consider doing one without their assistance and now he and Victor are sharing their expertise with everyone.

As I read the newest version of *Acquiring More Profit* I again realized the importance of understanding the nuances of an acquisition. This book should be a must read for all Broker Owners as at one time or another you will be an acquirer or a seller. Knowing what is happening and why will make the transaction more successful and the entire process less stressful. I learned early on that the right third party doing the financial analysis and presentation of that analysis makes for a successful conclusion. I highly recommend George, the WAV Group, this book, and the *Acquiring More Profit Implementation System*. Get this book and use its concepts and tools to reach a successful transaction while saving you time, money, and a whole lot of stress."

Larry Rideout, Chairman & Owner

Gibson Sotheby's International Realty

"Finally, a comprehensive, evergreen and incredibly easy to digest blueprint for M&A success in the residential real estate space. I've experienced both sides of the process as an executive leader. The best advice I can offer is to conduct extraordinary research, be incredibly prepared and have a watertight implementation plan. This book is a stellar resource that will help you best accomplish those tasks."

Pat Shea, President & CEO

Lyon Real Estate

"This book is a must read for any and every broker owner in the business. Each chapter is relevant and insightful. Well done Victor and George!"

Lacey Merrick Conway, President & CEO

Latter & Blum

"George is a legend in the real estate valuation, mergers, and acquisitions space. Anytime we are doing anything big, I always make sure to discuss it with him. Now he, combined with Victor Lund are offering the benefit of their vast experience to everyone. This book and corresponding Implementation System are a complete master class on how to complete a successful M&A transaction."

Anthony Lamacchia, CEO

Lamacchia Companies, Inc.

"Acquiring (More) Profit is a comprehensive guide to mergers and acquisitions in the real estate industry, providing valuable insights and tools for successful transactions. The authors' extensive experience and emphasis on cultural compatibility and a "win-win" approach make this book a must-read for anyone considering an M&A strategy in the industry."

RJ Long, Managing Partner

Coldwell Banker Prime Properties

"This book is a must read for anyone contemplating buying, or even selling a real estate company. Creating a successful M&A strategy from prospecting to closing is introduced complete with explanations, examples, checklists, and forms. George and Victor offer a comprehensive guide that should be in every broker's resource library. I especially appreciated their take on the importance of cultural compatibility, understanding motivations, and maximizing the value for both sides which are critical concepts often ignored in our industry."

Gino Blefari

CEO | HomeServices of America, Inc.

Chairman Berkshire Hathaway Home Services

"A broker's responsibility is to implement, not create; this system allows the best of both. I have been using the concepts and tools in the original book successfully for over 20 years and have completed multiple acquisitions because of it. My go to resource for all things M&A has always been Acquiring Profit, it has been a major factor fueling our growth. Now with the updated book and this system, the process is easier than ever. In addition to always engaging George and the WAV Group, our company uses multiple tools offered in the book and The Acquiring Profit Implementation System on every M&A transaction."

Paul McGann, President & Owner

Gibson Sotheby's International Realty

"Just the name Acquiring Profit speaks volumes. The writing by George and Victor is the most comprehensive guide to Mergers and Acquisitions I have seen. A buyer or a seller could use this as a daily playbook going through the entire process. Although there is a process to M&A, being in the people business makes it all about the people - as a result every deal is slightly different. This book focuses heavily on the importance of creating a fair and beneficial transaction for both sides, a must I believe for a successful transaction."

Mark A. McLaughlin, President

McLaughlin Ventures

Former CEO, Pacific Union International

Contents

Introduction 10
Overview 13
Chapter 1: The Basics 16
Chapter 2: Getting Started 50
Chapter 3: Approaching a Candidate............................ 61
Chapter 4: Relationship-Building.................................. 82
Chapter 5: Information Gathering And Due Diligence 102
Chapter 6. Valuation And The Offer............................. 135
Chapter 7: Pre-Closing 177
Chapter 8: The Closing & Transition........................... 194
Chapter 9: Making It All Work 207

Buying Home Services Businesses................................... 218
Addendum A: Case Study — Move-in Acquisition...... 220
Addendum B: Case Study — Fold-In Acquisition 223
Glossary of Terms 228
Concluding Thoughts 235
Acknowledgments 236
About the Authors 237

Introduction

Since the first *Acquiring Profit* book was published, 25+ years have passed. In the age of pod-casts, real estate channels, e-books, and large amounts of information available instantly, I still get requests for the book. I often converse with company owners who still have a copy on their bookshelves and refer to it. For that I am both amazed and thankful.

Acquiring Profit was the first (and, I feel, still best) book dedicated to mergers and acquisitions, or M&A, in the real estate brokerage industry. The foundational concepts of the importance of cultural compatibility and a "win-win" approach to the transaction have withstood the test of time. Many of the industry players have changed over the years, and the decimal points on purchase prices have definitely moved significantly. However, much of the described M&A process and techniques written about in the original book are valid, and I still use them every day.

M&A activity has also survived the test of time by not slowing during the last few decades but actually accelerating. Growth through M&A has been the springboard for every large company's success in the industry.

So why write another book?

There has been so much I have learned since the original book's printing that, when I read it now, I think of all the things it is missing. Since it was published, I have literally worked on hundreds of transactions of all sizes, for almost every major brand, learning more on every one. I have wanted to write an update for many years because I knew about all of the expanded experiences, insights, checklists, and helpful hints that could and should be added.

I have for many years been aware of the tremendous appetite for real estate brokerage firm M&A information in our industry. There is still very little quality information available. If brokers were still referring to a 25-year-old book for assistance, I felt it extremely important to update and expand on the process, with improvements, as it is today. I was asked so often when I was going to update it, and I always put it off to do sometime in the future. Then I met Victor Lund.

I was very fortunate to join Victor and his wonderful wife, Marilyn Wilson, to start the M&A Advisory Division at WAV Group. For those of you who are not familiar, WAV Group is the preeminent real estate strategy and consulting group to the real estate industry. WAV Group has been either behind the scenes or out in front of many of the major industry initiatives, and major company events, of the past two decades.

Both of them encouraged me to update the book, as they had used it themselves in the past and heard regular requests for updates from many of their consulting clients. After much prodding, Victor even agreed to be a co-author. With no other excuses I could assemble, the information-gathering and writing journey began.

We both agreed that there was a good foundation in the original book, but there was so much more that could be included. We decided an update was not exactly what was needed, but instead decided to write a whole new book.

We wanted to share, in a new format, the collective knowledge and experiences of Victor, myself, and the many friends who have contributed. The one thing we did retain was the name ... sort of. We were adamant that *Acquiring Profit*, not just doing an acquisition, was the key concept we wanted readers to glean from the book. We also liked the name, so we landed on *Acquiring (More) Profit*.

We also had many checklists, forms, and agreements that really do not fit well because of size constraints in a normal book, but they are perfect for digital downloads and manipulation. We decided to create a supplement book with digital files, with forms and checklists that can be customized for individual firm needs. We are calling this the Acquiring Profit Implementation System and, it is a perfect complement to assist with the actual execution of your M&A strategy. It contains many valuable time- and money-saving tools, such as:

- Sample prospecting approaches
- An NDA
- LOI
- Contracts
- Transition Plans
- Plus all the checklists mentioned in this book and more

To order and receive more information on the Acquiring Profit Implementation System at www.wavgroup.com/amp.

Victor's industry insight, his M&A experiences, and his encouragement have been invaluable to the completion of this book. The acquisition or sale of a brokerage is as much about people and systems as it is about financials. Without Victor, this book would not be as weighted with valuable information — and it may have never been finished.

It is our hope that *Acquiring (More) Profit* will remain on your bookshelves or live in your computer for another 25 years and still retain its relevance.

George Slusser

Overview

With the purchase of this book, you have expressed an interest to learn more about the exciting world of real estate brokerage firm mergers and acquisitions (M&A). This pathway has been a significant growth strategy for most of the top real estate firms in the U.S. today.

Our vision was to explain the complete M&A process from A to Z so you can understand what others have done and then fairly determine whether it is the right approach for you, too. Ultimately, we hope you learn enough from this book to make the right decision for your company, and our success in meeting our vision will be judged by your actions.

Why consider a merger or an acquisition? M&A can allow your company to quickly add agents, increase market share, revenue, add management talent, and creative cost efficiencies for both your fixed and variable expenses.

Overall, M&A can be a complex and challenging process that requires careful planning and execution to be successful. The title of this book, *Acquiring (More) Profit*, conveniently sums up our philosophy. We have witnessed many M&A transactions that added revenue, added agents, increased market share, and expanded overall brand awareness — but, unfortunately, did not increase the company's profits.

We believe that, by far, the best way to grow a real estate company is through acquisitions .... but we want you to do it *profitably*. This philosophy is grounded in the concepts, stories, checklists, and recommended processes in the pages that follow.

We also believe that both the seller and buyer can greatly benefit from an acquisition; there does not need to be a winner and a loser. We will share the process of building trust between the parties, how best to find out the true motivations and needs of the seller, and the steps to creating a structure that shares the risk while maximizing the potential for both sides.

We also explore the concept that the purchase price and terms are not the most important contributor to a transaction's success. The most important component to success on both sides is cultural compatibility, which will be a thread through the entire process.

As you read this book, it will be important for you to carefully consider the potential benefits as well as the risks of an M&A strategy. There are several challenges that we will explore in depth to better explain the process of mergers and acquisitions (M&A).

Some of these challenges include:

1. **Prospecting:** Who are the potential targets, and how do we determine the best ones? Then, how do we approach them?
2. **Valuation:** Determining the fair value of the target company can be difficult, especially if the company has complex assets or liabilities, or if the market is rapidly changing.
3. **Integration:** Integrating the operations and cultures of two companies can be complex and time-consuming, and it may require significant resources and management attention.
4. **Communication:** M&A can involve a significant amount of change for employees and agents. Effective communication is critical to ensure that they understand the changes and how they will be affected.
5. **Purchase price:** Determining the correct purchase price, offer structure, and terms and conditions.
6. **Risk management:** M&A involves a certain level of risk, including financial, operational, and even risks to a company's credibility or reputation. These risks must be carefully managed to ensure that the transaction is successful.
7. **Cultural differences:** M&A can involve the integration of two companies with different cultures and ways of doing things, which can be a source of tension and conflict.

These are just a handful of the major areas we will discuss in-depth in the following chapters. We are offering in these pages the benefit of the collective knowledge and experiences that WAV Group executives have earned over decades of being involved in hundreds of M&A deals.

Even though every transaction is different, there are many similarities in the process. These patterns repeat themselves. The process is almost always the same, no matter the size of the firms, the market, or the participants. We hope to share with you the strategies that have been successful in our careers and to help you avoid the many mistakes we have made or witnessed others making.

Acquiring (More) Profit is a mindset that should feed your operational decision-making. When you are running a company, you always need to bear valuation in mind.

Chapter 1: The Basics

Vince Lombardi, the famous football coach of the Green Bay Packers, started every new training camp the same way: On the first day, at the first session, he began by holding up a ball and telling the team, "Gentlemen, this is a football." Lombardi wanted all to know that he was committed to preparing his players as thoroughly as possible to win.

Although being successful in the merger-and-acquisition M&A) arena takes a different talent and effort, we too want you to be as thoroughly prepared for success as possible. Hence, we will start at the beginning: explaining what exactly an M&A opportunity is and how to achieve success.

If you are going to employ an M&A growth strategy by joining forces with another company, the first thing you must decide is whether to *merge* with another company or to *acquire* it. Almost every real estate press release touting the merger of two great firms in the past 30 years has announced that company A has merged with company B. Interestingly, many in real estate (including us) use the term "merger" to describe what is essentially an acquisition.

The term "merger" is preferred because it is not helpful to the agents, or their clients, to believe that the firm is going away. "Merger" is a gentler term that postures two great companies coming together to deliver something better than before. Although the terms "merger" and "acquisition" are often used interchangeably, there are important technical differences.

An acquisition occurs when one entity purchases controlling interest in another and is absorbed into that entity. This typically means the old name goes away (but not always), there is new management making decisions, and the acquirer has 51% financial control of the entity or more.

We like to use the term "merger" for every transaction because it fits so well with our philosophy for a successful transaction. As mentioned above, it suggests a spirit of cooperation between the two parties involved; "acquisition," to some, may connote that one party is "taking over" the other. An acquisition that benefits both sides should be as friendly and cooperative as a merger, joint venture, or partnership.

Our book focuses primarily on how to conduct a successful acquisition, which is the most prevalent in the industry: Company A buying 100% of the assets or stock of Company B, and then calling it a merger. To make the landscape even more confusing, everything related to the acquisition process often is just called M&A. This has become the standard "catch-all" phrase in the industry.

We believe most in the industry tend to approach both acquisitions and mergers from the wrong direction. Many in the industry view the M&A process as primarily a financial transaction (we do not); they assume if that they pay the owner enough, they will get the company, and the agents will willingly follow. This is not always the case, as we can tell you from experience.

We call agents leaving early after the closing "breakage." Minimizing agent defection and breakage is the key to a successful financial outcome for both the buyer and seller. We view the financial step as the *third*-most-important component for a reason (after competency and cultural compatibility). Most M&A discussions, material, and training are all about the financial side. We believe the finances can be worked out with a reasonable and responsible seller or future partner if the competency, culture, value proposition, and timing align well.

WHAT IS A MERGER?

A merger of two corporations typically involves the transfer of stock of both corporations, with a formation of a new entity. Along with the transfer of ownership, there is typically a sharing of the responsibilities involved in the management control changeover.

Generally speaking, with a merger you are taking on a full or limited partner, one who is likely to become part of the decision-making process at the new company. Obviously, in such a situation, an owner is giving up some level of control over the business.

Why would you choose to take this route? It could be that you desire or need a partnership, for a number of reasons as outlined in the table below.

For example, an owner may be in need of management help and support. The owner may be strong in one management aspect, (such as sales management) but weak in another area (such as recruiting). Or the owner may enjoy training and mentoring agents but dislike dealing with all the marketing, financial, and operational sides of the business.

A partner who has complementary strengths may be the missing link to grow both companies and make them more profitable. That partner may be able to relieve some of the decision-making burdens, provide a second voice and perspective, and help make the tough choices and share the hard work. In such a scenario, if you can find a truly compatible partner, then a merger can be an outstanding opportunity. There are many such successful partnerships around the country, and they typically involve partners who work well together, share a common vision, and also complement each other's skill sets.

In evaluating a merger partner, it is best to determine what you are hoping to gain. You must look inward and answer a number of questions:

- What are your current weaknesses? What are your strengths?
- What brokerage activities do you enjoy, and which are your least favorite?

- Are you compatible with the owner, the culture they have created, and their view of the industry?
- Will a merger accelerate what you are hoping to accomplish with your firm and career?
- Is this the right partner for you and your agents?
- What will be the true synergies and cost savings?
- What does the new pro-forma budget look like?
- Is there an acceptable alternative to growing your firm? What are the costs and benefits to taking that alternative?

MARGIN IMPROVEMENT AND PROFITABILITY

There may also be financial reasons behind choosing some form of an M&A.

If, for example, your profits have plateaued, and yet you need to raise capital for continued growth and investment, a merger may make sense. In effect, a merger allows you to trade off a certain amount of stake in ownership for an infusion of resources — agents, listings, facilities, cash flow, and perhaps expertise — that can help "jump start" your company. A merger can be a quick boost to top-line revenue and instantly increase earnings.

Two companies that are not dropping much money to the bottom line individually, when combined, can reach profitability quickly. Both provide services to their agents and incur fixed expenses that often have much excess capacity.

Some examples could include a staff person who is supporting 7 agents and who could support 15, or empty or unused office space that could support additional agents. A merger should provide immediate synergies with the ability to eliminate duplicate expenses. This increase in efficiency combined with a better utilization of existing fixed expenses allows the profit margin to, potentially, grow exponentially.

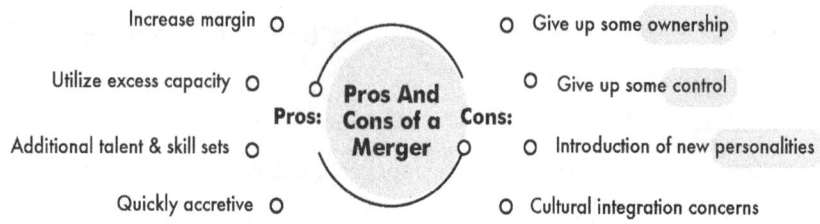

GIVING UP CONTROL

Keep in mind that when you give up ownership by way of a merger, you may be instantly losing something that is very important to you — the ability to control your own destiny. It may be something as small as being questioned about an expensive dinner you had at a conference or something as prominent as the company's branding and messaging.

"The issue of control is the central question when deciding between a merger and acquisition," says acquisitions expert Dr. Steve Franklin of Global Access Learning. As Franklin notes, a merger may necessitate that you now collaborate and negotiate with your new partner on everything from internal policy matters (such as commission splits) to the sharing of expenses and even the name of the company.

This can be a problem for many real estate brokers, who are used to being entrepreneurs and running their own show. Chances are good that they have spent years growing a team and shaping a culture that reflects their own philosophy. They also may enjoy certain freedoms of ownership; because the real estate business often tends to combine work and personal life, some brokers may be used to going on trips and paying for it through the company, or expensing their car payment, or giving a family member a salary (for little or no work) — all out of the company's revenue. When you take on a partner, be prepared to answer for all of the expenses; everything should be (and must be) explained.

Those who do opt for a merger partnership should be very careful about who they choose as a partner. If there is a potential for conflict between partners, it is likely to be exacerbated in a post-merger environment. Because you do not really get a chance to learn and grow with your partner, all of a sudden you have a good-sized company to run, and you'll have to make major decisions together. It is important to spend a lot of time together and research any "what-ifs" upfront before they happen, including the scope of the business plan and the division of responsibilities, to avoid misunderstandings and conflicts.

Beyond these operational and monetary issues, you should have a sense of how the personalities and cultures of the partners will mesh. It is important to have in-depth pre-merger meetings and discussions, always looking for common ground and areas where you are *not* aligned. It is always — we repeat, *always* — suggested to create an effective buy-sell agreement that's negotiated and signed prior to the merger. This is critical to establishing a mutual vision, commitment, and an effective partnership upfront. Hopefully this document will never have to be used, but it gives both sides comfort that if the occasion arises, for whatever unforeseen reason, there is a way out.

We created the following merger discussion document to assist with the evaluation process.

Merger Discussion Format

(This format also works well for acquisitions.)

1. Confidentiality

    a. Who is allowed to know about this?

    b. Who is specifically *not* allowed to know? What happens if (when) the word gets out? What is the desired messaging?

2. Non-disclosure agreement (NDA) — create and execute based on confidentiality parameters

3. Begin with the end in mind: Individual questions for principal M&A participants:

    a. Vision for the future — what does the combined firm look like in one year? Three years? Five years?

b. What does success look like for each principal? Can you quantify how you will measure success?

c. What lines of business, market share, volume, and earnings are currently feasible? What could the merger or acquisition add to the business?

d. How much time do you want to devote to this entity? This year, in year three, and in year five?

e. When would you like to begin to decrease your workload?

f. What role would you see yourself filling? This year, in year three, and in year five?

g. How do you want to be compensated?

h. How do you expect to be paid?

i. What is your ideal exit strategy?

j. What is the best entity structure for each principal?

k. Is there a shared business philosophy or culture? Can you define it?

l. How many hours will you plan to work each week after the merger?

m. How much vacation time do you expect after the merger? When do you expect to take it?

4. Current needs analysis and discussion

   a. Individual firm strengths
   b. Individual firm challenges
   c. Principal strengths
   d. Employee and agent strengths and weaknesses
   e. Competitive advantages
   f. Are there unfulfilled markets, unexplored verticals, or other potential for growth?
   g. What future needs must be met to remain competitive and thrive?

5. SWOT analysis: Internal and competitive comparison

   a. Strengths (for each company and for primary competitive players in the market)

   b. Weaknesses (for each company and for primary competitive players in the market)

   c. Opportunities (for each company and for primary competitive players in the market)

   d. Threats (for each company and for primary competitive players in the market)

6. Expectations of merger: personal and business

   a. Preliminary job descriptions of principals

   b. Work schedule and type of activity expected

   c. Business location — now, in three years, in five years

   d. Name and branding

   e. Future business expansion — when and where

   f. Pace of growth

   g. Appetite for additional investment and cash calls

7. Information-gathering-exchange: The due diligence suggested

   a. Tax returns for past two to three years

   b. Firm P&L statements and balance sheets (past three years)

   c. Long-term and short-term debt ledgers

   d. Outstanding expenses (unpaid bills)

   e. Business-line revenue and expense statements, if available

   f. Depreciation schedules

   g. Organizational charts, if available

   h. Employee summary, with duties and earnings for last three years

   i. Agent summary of the previous three years, with earnings

   j. Owner's compensation analysis for previous three years

k. Assets to come with the merger; will any be specifically excluded?

   l. Policy and procedures handbooks: review and revision

   m. Summary of agent support offerings (and who pays for what)

   n. Special agent compensation arrangements, if different than handbook

   o. Active leases or contracts

   p. Memberships and associations — fees, obligations, and benefits

   q. Current listing inventory, with expiration dates and fee to firm

   r. Current pending sale inventory, with fee to firm

   s. Current management compensation summary, with monthly fee, responsibilities, and term

   t. General insurance policies

   u. E&O policy

   v. Litigation pending — three-year summary

   w. Technology tools and assessment of hardware and software solutions

   x. Social media presence and offerings

   y. Marketing and training materials, including agent hiring and onboarding standards and policies

8. Company comparisons and preliminary discussion: What and whom to keep

   a. Commission schedule

   b. Administrative support

   c. Technology support

   d. Policy and procedures manual

   e. Who pays for what: Car/mileage, business expenses, signs, cards, marketing materials, training, meetings, and more — both for principals and agents

   f. What is the individual philosophy on advertising and marketing?

g. Office space — now and future

h. Accountant and legal services: Current support and future needs projections

i. Culture — meeting frequency, dress code, agent expectations for production and effort

9. Financial valuation

   a. Review existing firm financials (profit-and-loss statements) for year-end 2021, 2022, and 2023, with time for Q&A

   b. Outside valuation conducted on both firms

   c. Determine true net value of each firm

   d. Are there any potential synergies and cost savings? People, support such as technology, websites, phone systems, space, and more

   e. Current contractual obligations — amount, term and benefit

   f. Create first year pro forma budget of merged firms

   g. Create shell of second and third budget — revenue amount and sources, major expense increases

   h. Identify initial contribution of each firm based on valuations

   i. Explore equal vs. unequal ownership options

   j. Decide: What is a fair merger from a financial standpoint as well as the resources each firm is "bringing to the table"?

   k. Letter of intent or term sheet — should include:

   l. Assets of the firms merging

   m. Firm expected contributions

   n. All pertinent deal points

   o. Expected close date

   p. Each firm is responsible for own attorney consulting fees, unless otherwise agreed

   q. Existing business treatment: revenue and expense reports (pending sales, listings, and management contracts)

r. The letter of intent or term sheet is non-binding; additional diligence is required

s. Formal contract to be prepared by X date — principals will hold each other to this obligation

10. Legal, tax, and financial details

    a. Entity type
    b. Ownership structure
    c. Buy/sell agreement
    d. Key person insurance
    e. Tax treatment
    f. Initial and ongoing cash contributions

11. Integration plan checklist (pre-closing)

    a. New entity business plan completed
    b. Transition budget created
    c. Facility issues finalized
    d. Human resource plan built
    e. Equipment/resource reallocation plan made
    f. Marketing plan constructed
    g. Buy/sell agreement finalized
    h. If new business name: Plan generated for signs, website, brochures, tools, other branding supplies
    i. Public relations plan (includes past clients)
    j. Transition advisory team created
    k. Kick-off and integration plan completed

12. Impact day (post-closing)

    a. Agent notification
    b. Client notification
    c. Industry and general public notification

d. Set consistent management meetings

   e. Set consistent transition advisory team meetings

Given the concerns of control and many instances of failed partnerships, it is not surprising that most owners of real estate companies would prefer to hire managers or acquire talent rather than consider partnering with another company. This is the reason why acquisitions tend to be the preferred growth strategy for many brokers.

In subsequent chapters, we will be primarily discussing acquisitions rather than mergers. Always keep in mind that using the term "merger" is usually a better positioning strategy. The positive mindset of the owner, agents, and staff derived from joining forces is usually better than the thought of being "bought out," acquired, or absorbed.

Acquisition

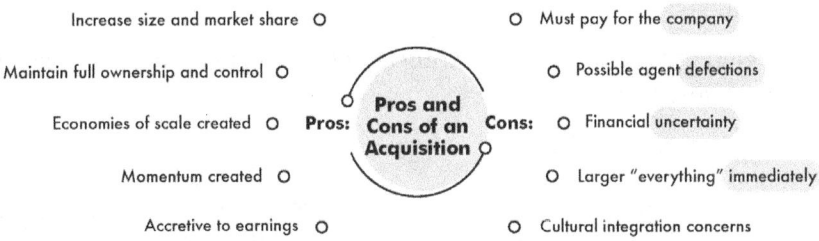

The seller has poured their life and heart into building their company. They do not want to appear to have failed or "sold out." Allow them to tell all their friends that they merged with the outstanding ABC Realty: "Now we are double the size and able to offer so much more!"

It is also easier for the seller to position a new partnership as a merger to their agents. It is much easier and more positive to say, "We have merged with ABC Realty, and now we are able to accelerate our growth plans and build an exciting company together. It is going to be a tremendous opportunity for us all."

Contrast that statement with telling the agents or community, "I am really tired of the business, so I decided to sell, and ABC was willing to buy." It is a totally different positioning of the same event.

Taking the time early on to discuss and set expectations across the board, from financial to cultural and beyond, can save you endless headaches later in the process.

Creating an Acquisition Strategy

There are two burning questions all company owners must answer.

- First, how can I best generate revenue and profitability for my business?
- Second, how do I maintain my profit and continue to grow my business?

We only know of three ways to grow:

1. Recruit new agents — and, hopefully, most of your recruits will be productive.
2. Organic growth through existing agents doing more transactions or increasing their price points.
3. Mergers and acquisitions

In our view, M&A is a very similar process to recruiting individual agents; you're just recruiting an owner with multiple agents all at once. It is relatively simple to understand, but it's not easy to do. (Actually, none of the choices are easy, but all can work, and many brokers are successful at growing through implementing all three.)

If you feel that growth through M&A is potentially the right path for you, we recommend committing to an acquisition strategy. This means spending time and financial resources to create a well-considered plan to grow your company through M&A.

First, you must internally debate what you hope to accomplish with an acquisition. Is your goal to prop up a struggling office, expand into a new market, gain additional market share at a certain price point, or is a combination of factors driving your exploration? Ultimately, we believe the best (and, indeed, only) reason to grow is the desire to increase profitability.

We have worked with some clients who happen upon an "opportunistic" acquisition. This may come about through befriending a competitor; after years, one day you might receive a call asking if you would be interested in buying their company. This is definitely not the norm, but even though it's not likely, it still happens.

Usually, this opportunistic acquisition is, in a way, using hope as a strategy approach. We have seen this type of acquisition work out well *if* the acquiring firm is prepared adequately for an unpredicted business-altering event.

We have also worked with clients who have told us that the acquisition they felt was too good to be true when it fell into their laps was, in effect, not as good as they had hoped. With this type of acquisition opportunity, you have to follow the same process of due diligence as you would for any other acquisition, skipping the prospecting part.

Conversely, a strategic or intentional approach, which we recommend, will provide you with many M&A opportunities if done correctly. The discussions that follow will work well in both situations if the process is followed.

The Two Types of Acquisitions

Assuming you want to proceed with an acquisition rather than a merger, you will likely choose between two different types of acquisitions:

- The first kind involves the assumption of an existing operation; we refer to this as a "move-in." In this type of acquisition, you would keep the seller's offices open, retain the agents, probably keep most of the staff, and usually (but not always) continue to offer any support services that agents are used to. In effect, you would move into the office and change the branding.

- The second type of acquisition is known as a "fold-in" or "roll-in." In a fold-in, you would close down a seller's existing operations and acquire the agents. You would then integrate and move those new agents into one of your existing offices or virtual platform. .

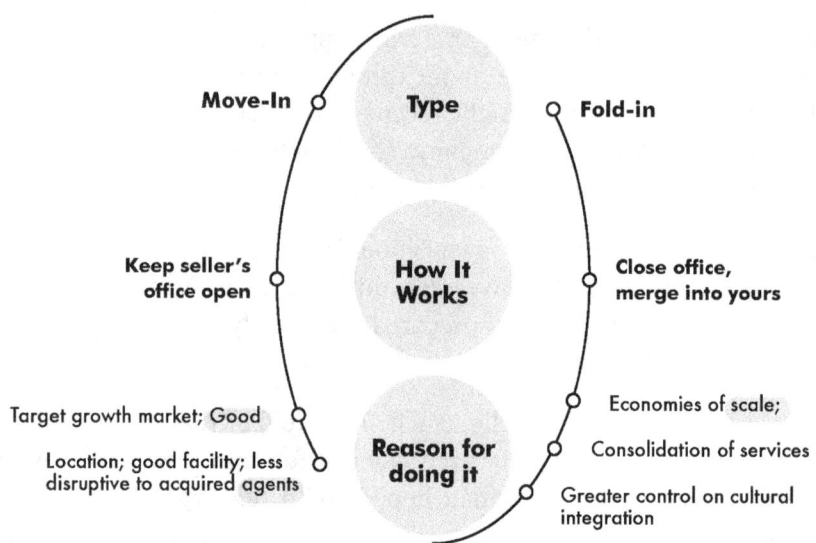

Even if your company has a strong, success-oriented culture, it may be difficult to instill that culture into a remote office. After the acquisition, the new agents may continue to operate for a long time by doing things the way they are used to doing them. That can quickly degenerate into an "us-vs.-them" situation (as can happen with any company branch office that is not considered "the main office").

Beyond that, the process of assuming existing operations inherently carries greater financial risk. There are occupancy and fixed expenses that you will be taking on. You will be under pressure to recruit and grow the top line to both pay for the acquisition and increase your profitability. When you assume existing operations, there is less opportunity to consolidate and eliminate duplicate expenses. On the contrary, you may find overhead costs soaring as you try to get the "new to you" office up and running at full speed.

Benefits Of A Move-In

There are reasons why it might be to everyone's advantage to maintain the existing office of the acquired company.

Location and space availability are probably the most important factors: If the office is in a prime location, an outstanding facility, or located in a market that you want to further develop, it would make sense to keep the office open. You may have existing agents that you could place in the office, or agents you would be able to recruit if you had an office in that location. Placing some of your existing agents in the acquired office also helps with the assimilation and integration of the new agents into your culture.

The primary challenge with a "move-in" is that changing the signs may not be all that is required to be successful at that location. If the company is selling to you because they are not making enough money (which is more than likely), then you will need a strong and expedient plan for growing the office. This will most likely be accomplished with a combination of recruiting new agents and organic growth of the existing ones.

There is also something to be said about not disrupting the agents who are used to working in that office. For many, the office is their work home. When the new owner arrives and does not disrupt their comfort, they are more likely to remain with the firm and give the new owner an opportunity to demonstrate why opportunity at the firm is the same as — if not better than — before the acquisition.

The Fold-In Trend

Fold-ins are becoming increasingly common as more large companies expand their footprints, provide large regional offices, or offer remote access. With shrinking brokerage company margins, "fold-ins" can more quickly accrue earnings for all parties. This app roach also minimizes the risk of taking on more fixed expenses while utilizing potential excess office, staff, and/or management capacity.

There are other reasons to opt for a fold-in, especially in your first (or first few) acquisitions. Typically, you can have much better control over the integration and assimilation of the two cultures. Momentum and enthusiasm can be quickly generated with an influx of new agents into an office. With the new agents unified and under closer watch, you can spot problems sooner, identify agents who need assistance with the transition, and see how agents are supporting the new direction.

A fold-in can often be a more complicated and demanding acquisition. The negotiating process may be more complex because the seller may have a facility, equipment, and other assets that are being left behind. You may be required to assist in the disposition of assets or sub-leasing of the facility. We will address this as an opportunity to differentiate yourself from other prospective buyers in later chapters.

A fold-in also can be disruptive to both the agents you are acquiring and your existing agents. Change is sometimes hard to accept. We have heard stories of agent rebellion for changes as minor as the coffee provider in the office. If your facility is not comparable (or perceived as better), does not offer the same support or services, or if the closing location is in a different geographic area, the seller's agents may begin to look elsewhere. You will have to communicate a compelling reason for a longer drive or perceived reduction in quality of facility or support.

In some ways, the agents who change offices are jolted into the benefits of change and are often reinvigorated in their work. Agents who have learned the skills of adaptation and have the capacity for fast change will likely become great producers.

Don't Shy From A Challenge

There are ways to resolve these potential conflicts. In general, acquisitions are not as difficult or costly as you might think. Do not let the word (or us!) scare you. While some people assume that acquisitions can only be understood by lawyers or financial experts, that is truly not the case. You may need some help along the way — for example, some legal advice when drawing up the contract, or valuation assistance when determining a fair offer — all of which is readily available. It can be a good idea to seek out a fellow broker who has completed or more acquisitions for advice. But most of the process can be done face-to-face between the buyer and seller, without anyone else involved. The process is very similar to recruiting an agent.

Please do not think you are unable to consider an acquisition because of limited resources, either. In the early days of real estate firm acquisitions, most of the purchase price, if not all of it, was paid upfront; buyers quickly learned that sellers could and would open another company and then whisk away agents and customers, or a large group of agents would leave and the buyer would be left with the shell of the company they just bought.

With that in mind, current purchases of real estate firms tend to be based on a deferred payout structure that maximizes the seller's payout in a shared-risk scenario. We'll share much more in later chapters about negotiating terms. So you do need *some* cash and reserves — but maybe not as much as you think.

Art vs. Science

The acquisition process is an art as well as a science, and in fact, it is more art than science. There is not always a consistent consensus around what a company is worth. We will show you formulas and how to apply them, but there are many factors that determine the ultimate purchase price.

Most important of all are the terms, followed by how well the firm fits the buyer's needs and wants, the market, the quality of the earnings, and many other variables tied to the uniqueness of the buyer and seller.

Remember: a brokerage is a people business, and the agents are independent contractors who can walk out the door more easily than you can recruit them. In any acquisition, comforting the agents and delivering business continuity with the understanding that their business will improve as a result of the merger is key! Mergers also spark an enormous recruiting opportunity.

There are specific steps and guidelines you can follow. Again, in some ways, an acquisition or merger is just like recruiting individual agents

– each case is different, but the most successful brokers tend to follow a process. In the many acquisitions we have been involved in we have developed a process that applies to almost any acquisition. Obviously, there are many components to the process, but they can be categorized into the following 10 steps that we used in the original book.

1. Research & identify quality candidates.
2. Establish contact with those candidates.
3. Build a relationship and analyze the needs and motivations of the candidate.
4. Gather information and perform diligence on the company.
5. Evaluate the company – both financially (valuation) and in terms of potential fit (cultural compatibility) with your own company.
6. Determine a purchase price and terms to be offered creating a letter of intent (LOI) and presenting the combined new company vision.
7. Develop a transition plan, pro-forma, and new budget.
8. Create purchase agreement, resolve contingencies, and close.
9. Integrate the two companies by executing the transition plan, with particular emphasis on the first 90 days.
10. Evaluate your results; adjust; return to step one and begin anew with your next acquisition.

In the following chapters, we will break down each of these steps in detail. We have also added sections on succession planning, when to consider selling your own company, and determining what strategy is right for you to grow your company.

Remember, an acquisition process may take one month or a few years; we've found that most acquisitions happen in a period of three to four months, once talks become serious on both sides. However long it takes, you almost always have to go through the above 10 basic steps, without skipping any of them. These steps will guide you through the journey in a logical and orderly fashion, helping you arrive at your ultimate goal — a successful and profitable acquisition.

PLANNING FOR A SUCCESSFUL EXIT

Often, I am asked: When is the best time to sell my real estate brokerage firm? The easy answer is, "When you do not need to." A better answer is, "When you are ready and it is a planned event.

The ideal time to sell your company is when your firm is positioned correctly to convey its value. Even more important is the timing: Ideally, you can sell your brokerage when it is in your best interests as a career or life decision. Buyers seek out and pay premiums for well-run, quality firms — and those are rarely for sale. You want to be one of those firms and ready when the time is right.

Is It The Right Timing?

My belief is that an exit strategy evaluation should be an important part of your annual business plan. Many owners only consider exiting when their profits are not consistently high enough for the amount of effort that running the firm requires. An unexpected exit may be the right timing from a life or career alternative standpoint.

However, even if you exit early, an exit preparation will allow you to receive maximum value for your firm. An unplanned or accelerated exit scenario is typically much better for the buyer than for the seller.

The terms "exit strategy" and "succession planning" are often used interchangeably. They can be one and the same, but succession planning is usually a process facilitating the owner's departure or retirement, with a planned transition to internal candidates. Having potential internal buyers or external candidates is always a good idea. I have worked with firms that knew five years ahead of time who they were building their firm to sell to — and then did it successfully.

Begin the plan with some honest self-reflection about your future. This can be simple notes or, as I suggest, a formalized process and clear strategy on when and how you might exit. Some work will be required, but it will be profitable time spent setting direction for your business. Most improvements you make to your business will be beneficial for you and a prospective buyer.

A very important consideration is a time frame. It is a "best practice" when doing budgets to look out at least three years (some firms do five). Much changes in our industry in three years, and it represents a fair target that needs less adjustments along the way. Ask yourself questions such as:

- Where do you want your firm to be in three years?
- What will the firm look like, and what do you need to do to get there?

Follow this by being truthful about when you see yourself doing something different: in 5 years, 20 years, 6 months? Please know that many buyers will want the owner to stay on to assist with the transition. I have seen the timeframe as short as 60 days, but more common is a schedule of 2 years or more. This extra time needs to be factored into your timing of doing something else after the sale.

Tracking The Value Of Your Firm

You need to operationalize and utilize an M&A mindset in your daily decisions. An important benchmarking tool is to have a professional valuation prepared on your firm so you have a realistic starting point.

A valuation will allow you to gauge how a potential buyer will perceive your firm's value today. If your desire is to get triple your current value, this can be your three-year goal (or longer).

Next, use your normal business planning process to determine how best to get there. Many firms receive valuations annually to confirm if they are on the right track.

Even if you are many years away from a potential exit, the exercise is a healthy one. Imagine you are going to sell in three years — what would you do differently? Clean up your accounting systems, make changes you have been contemplating for years, close or consolidate a branch office?

Growing your firm to maximize profitability is essentially the same as positioning it for sale in three years. Buyers will not typically give you much credit for infrastructure or personnel investments that you have made that do not yet reflect improved profitability. It may take one to two years for an investment today to be fully realized in profitability. If you want to grow your firm by 3X, then it will take an investment (time or money), prioritized improvements, an implementation plan, execution, and adjustments along the way.

If circumstances in year two or three cause an early sale, you are still in a much better position. You have already made improvements and are in the proper mindset of a planned event. Hopefully, at the end of three years, you will have achieved your profitability goal and the investments have more than paid for themselves. You have maximized your value and made your firm a more attractive sale candidate. Congratulations!

If you are still years away from exiting, then start a new three-year plan with even higher target goals.

Many companies do a relatively poor job of keeping their firm in "sellable" condition. That is a mistake. Always keep the M&A mindset in your monthly, quarterly, and annual planning and reporting. If you were selling the company today, where is the weakness? What do I need to do to increase the firm's value to where I want it? Create and implment plan to fix whatever I needed to achieve your goals.

Create A Crisis Exit Plan

We all know unexpected events happen that can change our business (or life) quickly. The fear of crisis from incapacitation, death or disaster is the burden of ownership.

As a part of your operational strategy, it is beneficial to create a "crisis exit plan." Ask the uncomfortable question: What should your family do if something happened to you? Who would take over your business, short-term and long-term? This is not an enjoyable exercise, but it's better for all to discuss in advance.

Well-run companies have contingency plans, and you owe it to your family and agents to build one. A "crisis exit plan" can be used for an immediate need but should also be a part of your long-term exit strategy.

The development of a crisis exit plan takes a lot of time. You need to start with making sure that your ownership is properly organized in a trust. This is typically tied to your last will and testament.

Make sure that the trust is listed on all of your bank accounts. Organize your insurance documents. Keep a ledger of all of your contractual obligations — their terms, renewal notice dates, and pricing. Remember, in a transaction, every one of these will be reviewed, so you might as well have them handy.

Keep in mind that companies that are sustainable without the primary owner usually bring a premium price when the time comes to sell or merge. Continuously building your firm with an exit in mind is a healthy exercise. This strategy allows you the opportunity to sell when you want to, on your terms.

Why Do Owners Sell A Real Estate Company?

We want you to really understand why most real estate companies are sold. Many quality, well-run, profitable, large firms sold because the right offer came at the right time. They may have been not ready to sell, but the offer was too good to pass up.

However, this is not the case for a vast majority of the firms we have worked with. We believe that most people reading this book will not want to overpay for a firm, nor risk huge cash outlays for assets that may or may not come back to work for you the next day.

Below are most of the reasons why owners sell their firm, in our experience.

Why Sell A Real Estate Company? Top 10 Reasons

10. Recieve a strong offer

9. Agent attrition

8. Personal or legal problems

7. Desire access to better resources

6. Partnership trouble or dispute

5. Tired of balancing management with personal production

4. Ready to retire

3. Want to relocate or start a new career

2. Burnout

1. Not making enough money for the time and effort needed

The biggest underlying reasons why people sell a real estate firm is time and money. It's not that they are not making any money, especially in the markets of the last few years, but they are not making *enough* money for the time invested to produce it.

For example, they made much more money as a producer with a lot less "hassle" than as an owner of the company. Reasons 10 through 2 may be critical to their decision, but they are not the primary change motivators.

Another example: If they were making what they felt was enough money for the time invested, maybe the management hassles or partnership issues would not be as important.

This list will be important in determining a seller's motivation in a later chapter, but it's also useful when determining why you would buy the company as seen below.

What Are The Benefits Of An M&A Strategy?

Most firms have excess capacity—either in space, management, support, or all three. Many could increase their agent count by 50% to 100% and have no need to add more fixed expenses. Once fixed expenses are covered, incremental margins and profit improve dramatically.

M&A can be quickly accretive to earnings. You could add talent, management help, a trainer, expand your footprint, expand price points, or even your product type.

Agent loyalty can often be transferred if the assimilation is done well. We believe acquired agents are more loyal than pulling one agent at a time out of a firm, usually by offering more compensation. A huge benefit can be the former owner(s) as experienced management help, a sales trainer, or even as a producer.

Many times the former owner (if they stay) can become a positive influencer as they are aware of how difficult the owner's job is and will communicate any dissent in the ranks. (Especially if they are still receiving compensation via the earn-out.)

Why Buy A Real Estate Company? Top 10 Reasons

10. Increase visibility; add agents, listings, and signs

9. Add a niche specialty to your existing business

8. Add outstanding facilities or services

7. Eliminate a competitor

6. Inject new life and energy into your company (and maybe you)

5. Gain a presence or expand in a new market

4. Add management talent

3. Gain market share

2. Make more cost-efficient use of your existing resources

1. Increase profitability through the economies of scale

This may be obvious, but we want to emphasize that most firms sell because they are not making enough money for the time invested. We have talked with a number of firms (none we advised) that have bought real estate companies for reasons 2 through 10 above but failed to accomplish the primary objective by increasing profitability.

There are some who believe that you will achieve profitability when you reach some larger size, at an undefined point in the future. Unless you are a tech company trying to gain revenue exponentially (using other people's money), with little need for profit before you "cash out," we believe every real estate firm acquisition should be about enhancing the bottom line. The other reasons and attributes gained with an acquisition are also important, but they are just bonuses to the primary goal: acquiring more profit.

The Self-Assessment

Are you ready to complete a successful acquisition? The first step to any effective M&A strategy is conducting an honest internal assessment. The basic questions to be answered:

- Do you have the management skills and expertise that would persuade a seller to trust you to manage their agents?
- Do you have a location, tools, systems, a reputation, or brand that would be attractive to others?
- What is your value proposition to your agents and clients?
- Are you an attractive landing spot for the seller, and why?
- Your offer will need to be more than about the dollars; the agents will ask:
- How does this change affect me, and does it offer a better opportunity for my personal business?
- Is this the best place to be?

Agents will know they have to change their business cards and branding anyway, so you need to convince them, covertly or overtly, that they'll be happier staying than leaving.

If you are not able to convince the owner that the agents will be happy and prosper under the new arrangement, then you will probably not be able to consummate a transaction unless you pay 100% upfront. If you are currently not able to recruit agents — well, you will be challenged, and M&A will be harder; that's recruiting an entire company at once.

Wall Street-backed companies are able to pay a lot more cash upfront. They tend to focus more on the financial side of the transaction rather than hope the agents come along. They can take more risks — but I believe theirs is the totally wrong approach.

A majority of privately held company transactions are done with an earn-out over three to four years. For the seller to maximize their earn-out, they must believe that you will run their company as well as or better than they could. You will be well-served in this process to spend more time recruiting both the seller and their agents than debating a few basis points in the multiple.

It is always good to perform a SWOT analysis annually. Later, we discuss the one we use in evaluating candidates, but the traditional one below works well to get you started.

1. Strengths

- Things your company does well
- Qualities that separate you from your competitors
- Internal resources such as skilled, knowledgeable staff
- Tangible assets such as facilities, capital, brand, value proposition

2. Weaknesses

- Things your company lacks
- Things your competitors do better than you
- Resource limitations
- Unclear unique selling proposition/ current market position

3. Opportunities

- Underserved markets- geography or price point
- Few or weaker competitors in your area
- Market growth for your services
- Press/media coverage of your company

4. Threats

- Emerging competitors
- Changing regulatory environment
- Negative press/media coverage or market perception
- Commission compression

Capital And Time

Do you have enough money for a down payment, transition expenses, and the miscellaneous costs that always seem to arise? Although we have seen acquisitions completed with little money, it is always better to have sufficient staying power (reserves) should something unforeseen happen.

Determine what amount of capital is available to you to comfortably purchase another company and then integrate it. You should even budget for the process of evaluating candidates.

You may spend considerable money on the diligence and legal side only to fail to close the transaction. Many have told us that some of the best acquisition decisions they have ever made included deciding not to complete an acquisition: after conducting their diligence, they knew was not the right fit. In our experience, if it does not "feel right" pre-closing, it will usually feel worse after an unsuccessful transaction that costs you much more money.

Every growth strategy takes time and an extreme amount of effort. We wish there was an easy method to growing a real estate firm, but we have not found it. We believe that M&A is the quickest and most profitable avenue of growth, but it will take a concerted effort from the owner and staff to prospect, conclude, and assimilate a new firm.

Obviously, the time spent will be contingent on the size of the acquisition compared to your existing size, but it will take considerable time both before and after the closing.

What Are Your Needs?

Do you have excess capacity in your existing office(s)? Do you have support staff that is underutilized? Do you need more management help? Are you having trouble breaking into a nearby market?

Identifying what you want to accomplish with an acquisition is important. We submit that most successful acquisitions are intentional.

Both of us have worked on transactions that have been "opportunistic." They start in reverse order to the normal process — with a call from a seller saying, "Are you interested in my firm?" These typically (but not always) do not end well, as the firm may or may not meet your actual needs. You have a potentially willing seller, but you then must determine whether you are a willing buyer, and all the diligence we will discuss must be followed. Transactions that appear too good to be true usually are.

Buyer's Perspective: Getting Ready

1. Needs analysis?
2. Team talent and competency
3. Bandwidth
4. Strengths and weaknesses
5. Capital evaluation

6. Growth commitment
7. What help will you need?

Here is a great story, contributed by Mark McLaughlin from WAV Group's M&A team reflecting back on his acquisition of Pacific Union.

After starting my first residential brokerage business in Marin County, California, in 2006, we enjoyed 20 months of hyper-growth as a start-up only to get slammed by the September 2008 meltdown of the equities markets — The Great Recession!

Small boutique offices, highly qualified and nimble professional staff striving to make our real estate professionals as successful as possible — and a fiscal discipline required by a start-up without venture capital funding. In Q4 '08, revenues [GCI] fell by 40% and stayed there until March '09.

We developed a weekly fiscal focus that proved successful for the next decade. Every Friday at 5 p.m., I received a report on new listings, new escrows, closings, and a rolling 90-day cashflow forecast. We had no choice but to manage the survival of the business.

We closed the Pacific Union acquisition in August 2009. Our due diligence was all paper-based; it involved no face-to-face meetings with the management team. Our only interaction was with GMAC Home Services (then owned by Brookfield).

Once closed, I remember my first meeting with the then-CFO of Pacific Union. I asked, "how does cashflow look for the next 90 days?" We now own the business, doing $50 million in GCI with an annual run-rate net loss of $3.7 million.

They replied, "We don't worry about cashflow; GMAC writes all the checks."

I was clearly stunned and afraid.

That next day we implemented the exact same Friday 5 p.m. reporting system described above, and it continued for six hundred and twenty (620) Fridays until a year after we were acquired by Compass.

I share this because they are instruments needed in bad times as well as good times. They are the lifeblood of a brokerage business.

Here are many of the actions we executed on and that you may consider.

- We closed our HQ office. The HQ team worked in local branches near their homes.
- We routinely closed non-performing branch offices — especially in M&A situations.
- Expiring leases were typically vacated for 50% smaller offices.
- We eliminated the "training department" and made sure professional staff were experts on technology resources.
- We optimized professional staff levels based on agent-to-staff ratios and shared workload across offices.
- We annually reviewed every "consultant" relationship to reduce spend.
- Annual audits of technology users vs subscription to reduce spend.
- Annual audits of marketing and advertising programs to reduce spend.
- Annual audits of "misc." or "other" expenses to reduce spend.

What About the Market?

We are often asked questions such as, "What market conditions are best for an acquisition — when should I be most aggressive? Is it better to acquire in a down market or thriving one?"

The answer is always: It depends on the circumstances. With our suggested intentional acquisition strategy, you should come across opportunities in all types of markets. There are always advantages and potential challenges posed by the existing market conditions, no matter what those are.

Seasonality

Over the long term, the time of the year an acquisition occurs should have little impact on its success. However, depending on the deal terms, the target's market seasonality can have significant short-term implications if not accommodated.

An extreme example might be a firm located in a vacation or second home market that does a majority of business during the summer and "shoulder" seasons. We have worked with many similar firms that have little revenue during the winter months. Although the purchase price remains the same, the cash flow received as a buyer would be drastically different in January than in August.

In all situations, we strongly recommend plotting the firm's historical cash flow and then creating a monthly proforma for the coming years so there are no surprises.

The other area where seasonality can affect the company is in agent compensation. If the firm's commission plan is on a calendar year basis, then as the year progresses, the company dollar decreases as agents advance in their compensation threshold's or reach caps. The cash flow available may look a lot different near the end of the year in November and December than the first quarter of the next year.

We also caution buyers to closely review the agent compensation plan and agent activity as the year nears a close. Many commission plans have severe "roll-backs" at the end of the year, causing more agent defections in December and January than any other time of year.

Good Times

In an ideal situation you would find a willing seller at a fair price and have a three-to-five-year market that is active and vibrant. This situation allows the seller to receive most if not all of their earn-out, maximizing their sales price. It also allows the buyer to pay off the seller with the cash flow generated and quickly increase the net value of their firm.

We always promote the fact that the goal should be for the seller to receive their full payout. If this occurs, it is an outstanding transaction for both sides.

The downside of buying during the good times is that sellers may not be ready to fully enjoy their sometimes-newfound profitability. Some sellers may desire much larger down payments, raising the risk factor for the buyer if the market slows. As we will discuss in the valuation section, in a rising market, sellers typically want to only look at the previous year and feel that prior years should be discounted or not included at all. Most sellers quickly forget that the market does not go up forever.

The tough decisions in a valuation relate to determining whether the previous year(s) is an outlier, trend, or just a result of the entire market lift. Unfortunately, neither side knows what the future market velocity will be. Forecasting or timing the market as a seller and a buyer is a very difficult, if not impossible, process. The fairest payment structure is based on a purchase price that is founded on actual performance, minimizing the risk to the buyer and maximizing the benefit to the seller. This approach automatically reflects the ebbs and flows of the market for both sides. During the good times is when most companies that are inclined think and seek M&A opportunities.

Not-So-Good Times

Market shifts, slowdowns, corrections, or even worse — the headlines will be everywhere. The entire real estate industry will be concerned if not outright worried about what effect the national economy will have on sellers and buyers.

Many brokers will ask "what should or can I do to prosper in these uncertain times?" Most will have the proverbial "deer in the headlights" look, just waiting for whatever happens to happen. Your question to answer as a firm owner is, "do I attempt to grow, sell, or just stay the course?" "Is this the time to be aggressive or to pull back on my acquisition strategy?"

The most famous investor of our time, Warren Buffet, offered some sage advice that I believe applies to our industry when it slows. He said,

"Be fearful when others are greedy. Be greedy when others are fearful." Our take on the advice is that slow times can be the most opportune moments to look at expansion through M&A activity.

Many sophisticated acquirers will save cash during the good times, knowing that the opportunity will arise when "cash is king again." These savvy players know they will have little competition for sellers as the stock-exchange-owned companies traditionally take a "pause" on their M&A activity.

During a slowdown, many potential sellers kick themselves for not selling previously. They may worry about how long the current market downturn will last. Some might call them fearful. The reality is that a market downturn is still generating transaction velocity, just not the numbers of the previous strong years. There are still very profitable acquisitions to be made, especially with consolidation plays.

During the "great recession" of our lifetime, George helped his wife June's fine real estate company close on five acquisitions. All the firms were quality additions, with great ownership and agents who unfortunately did not have the staying power to continue operating independently. They were all of the "fold-in" variety, which immediately added revenue but only minimal additional expenses.

Her firm was the only major firm in the market to remain intact coming out of the recession, and she survived well. She is confident the acquisitions allowed the firm to emerge from the recession more quickly, far more profitably, and then to dominate in the markets served.

No one we know of is predicting a future slowdown or decline like we experienced in 2008 through 2010, but a similar dynamic is in play in a cooling market. Many brokers repeat the history of not creating enough capital reserves during the good times, or they are not able to reduce expenses quickly enough to maintain profitability during the slower times.

Many new brokerages are started when times are good; some may not have had the time to save and may still be paying off start-up expenses. Brokers in these situations who are trying to determine their best next move are often great M&A candidates and are usually willing to discuss options.

Chapter 2: Getting Started

Identifying Candidates

Once you have determined that you have competency, capacity, and capital for an acquisition strategy, it is time to get started.

(We know that is what you have been waiting to hear, but we felt we needed to provide some background and caution before digging into the actual process. Now you're *really* ready!)

The first step is to identify companies that you might be interested in joining forces with. Sounds simple enough, but depending on your market, there may be many companies worthy of consideration.

We have often heard that "there is no one in my market I would want to acquire." People embarking on an acquisition strategy tend to make the mistake of ruling out potential candidates based on faulty assumptions. Don't assume, for example, that a company with a good reputation and strong track record would be unwilling to sell or would be unaffordable to you.

Also, don't exclude a company because of one bad agent interaction or something negative you have heard about them in the market. Most real estate agents are the same; it is just the training (or lack thereof) or tools, or even supervision that may have caused them to be sloppy in contract writing or get in trouble because they were not taught correctly.

If you rule out candidates in this manner, you may miss out on a great opportunity to provide a better future for them. We believe that apart from known ethical issues, you should consider almost everyone to be a potential candidate.

There will be some companies that will be under agreement with a brand and may not be able to sell at this time. But now is the time in this process to "plant the seed" in their minds that you are a very qualified option for them when their agreements eventually expire. We have done transactions with quality firms that we talked with five years before the deal closed; they were interested, but it was just not the right time because of their existing agreements or other issues.

As we discussed in the previous chapter, the primary reason companies sell can often be traced to a failure to make enough money for the time invested. You may find the smaller firms in your market with an owner in personal production are having a hard time recruiting or keeping pace with larger competitors. Sometimes mid-sized companies are literally "caught in the middle" not able to offer all the services or economies of scale of larger companies, but not aided by the personal production of the owner anymore. What about larger companies?

Bigger Companies May Be Candidates

Do not assume that you can only acquire a company that is smaller than yours. There have been cases of companies acquiring firms twice or more their size. A large firm may not have a good succession option identified, and perhaps key stakeholders are ready to retire, or the timing is just right for them to depart the business. You will never know unless you ask!

A larger company may also consider selling a branch or two that has under-performed or that is not in their primary market anymore. Large companies can also struggle financially.

This does not mean that a candidate must be in deep financial trouble before they'll be willing to sell to you. A company may actually be doing well, but as we stated previously, there are other factors at play influencing the decision. Obviously, the advantage of acquiring a company that is doing well financially is that you know there is great potential for that operation to continue to be profitable for you, without requiring a major overhaul.

Conversely, you might find the best opportunities, price-wise, can be found among companies that are struggling — but that have the potential to perform better under your leadership. A company in need can represent the best opportunity, provided you have the ability to change, motivate, and improve the operations.

There have been many instances where a company was under-capitalized, or it lacked the leadership, training, or tools to prosper. After the acquisition by a well-run, quality firm, the agents blossomed.

It is important not to rule out marginal candidates (in your view) because of their size or past sales performance; as long as the company is ethically sound, they should be considered a potential candidate.

A common practice among large enterprise firms is to organize their offices in regions and assign a regional manager to lead it. Additionally, enterprise firms operate a construct of looking at offices or regions as "core" vs. "challenger."

Core markets are areas where they have market stability and strong, sustainable transaction volume. Challenger markets are areas where they may not have sustainable transaction volume, but they have a strategy to grow the business. And sometimes, offices are there simply to support the lifestyle of the owner.

A popular example of "lifestyle" offices are companies in the midwest or northeast that have an office or two in Florida or Arizona. An example of a strategic office is a San Francisco Bay Area company that has an office in Lake Tahoe or Carmel — popular vacation spots for clients and agents in their core markets. And sometimes, companies open offices in expansion areas that simply don't make it — maybe they have the wrong manager or some other flaw in their growth strategy.

These are all good examples of acquisition targets when the timing is right.

Finding A Niche

You may choose to look for candidates within a particular niche, such as a pure property management firm, if your goal is to strengthen a specific aspect of your company or expand into a new area.

There are any number of potential compatible niche markets, such as:

1. Luxury homes
2. New home sales
3. Commercial and investment real estate
4. Condos
5. Waterfront properties
6. Property management and rentals
7. Resort properties
8. Development
9. Timber
10. Agriculture or ranch Land

As you can see from the list, there are many niche possibilities that could add to your business model.

Remember as you seek out candidate firms that you do not necessarily need to acquire an entire company. There is also the option of acquiring a "company-within-a -company."

We are seeing many cases where agent *teams* are being acquired in the same manner as an entire company. A lead agent may have five or fifty agents working for them. The acquisition process is very similar to an entire company, and sometimes even easier. The lead agent(s) may have more control over their team members and sustainable production than a company owner has over all of their agents.

Sources Of Information

When investigating the reputations of companies and whether they would be a viable candidate, there are many people that may offer help.

By talking with your own agents, you can find out a lot of things you may not already know about other companies or their agents in the market. Your agents have hopefully had co-op experiences with the agents from firms you are researching.

You can also talk with knowledgeable suppliers to the industry, such as people at:

- MLS data providers
- Mortgage companies
- Banks
- Insurance companies
- Attorneys
- Escrow companies
- Sign installers
- Market websites and magazines
- Board staff

Suppliers and vendors to the industry tend to know quite a bit about the reputation and workings of particular brokerages. They may be able to determine if a company is not doing well financially due them being a "slow pay," someone key to the business success nearing retirement, or an owner who's just ready to get out.

Your agents can get involved by spreading the word throughout the market that you are looking to expand. It is a healthy and prideful feeling for agents to know their company is doing well and wanting to expand — but only with quality additions.

Non-Candidates

Is there anyone that should not be considered a candidate? Probably the only companies that you should automatically steer clear of would be those that are not ethically sound.

If the company has a bad reputation, do your diligence to make sure that reputation is deserved. If the reputation is based on actual behavior, then such an alliance could tarnish your brand. Even if acquired for free, this company could cost you in lost clients and possibly some of your existing agents.

Please do keep in mind that, occasionally, agents with a struggling company get an unfair rap due to one example of ego clashes with agents or a disgruntled client. Try to confirm that the poor reputation is legitimate.

Remember that if the agents are fundamentally sound and will take direction and meet your expectations and standards for behavior, the old company's reputation quickly dissipates. It is the individual agents that will make your acquisition a good decision or not.

The other type of company that is normally not a great candidate is one locked into a long-term agreement. Many franchise agreements last for 10 years. Do not assume that there is no "out" in their agreement, or how much time is remaining. Just know that this is something to discuss early in the process — and even if they really want to sell, you do not want to interfere with any contractual obligations they are committed to.

Please also know that we have acquired firms three to five years after our initial discussions with them by keeping in contact and letting them know we are interested before they are able to sell. Think of your targets as a sales funnel — some are long-term and some are short-term. But always invest your time in developing those acquisition relationships and developing goodwill.

As you begin to consider all the possible candidates in your market, remember there is no harm in inquiring about a firm and asking if they are interested in a merger or sale as long as you inquire properly.

You will find that most people are curious what you are up to and why you are interested in their company. They have probably been approached by some of the large nationals or regionals in the past if they have a good company, but maybe not a quality up-and-coming firm like yours. At the very least, you might make a new friend. As hockey great Wayne Gretzky once said, "You miss 100% of the shots you don't take."

And remember, no brokerage owner is going to ever answer your call and say, "Yes, I would love to sell." All you are looking for is an opportunity to meet to determine if there is any opening to work together. If a rumor gets out that a company is for sale, you can watch the agents walk out the door, so starting with a quiet discussion is usually the best approach.

Beginning The Search

At this point, you have hopefully determined that there are potential sellers all around you — but how do you let these people know that you are a potential buyer? If you are serious about finding the best acquisition candidate, you must establish an identity among these potential candidates; it must be clear to them that your company is interested in growth through acquisitions.

We have seen companies sell to a national firm (us, many times) and the local market did not know they were for sale. When asked by friendly competitors in the market why they were not contacted, the seller often will say "I am sorry; I did not know that you would be interested."

That is the truth the seller believed as the competitor never expressed an overt interest. You want to become not only an option, but the *best* option, now or in the future.

Candidates will often gravitate toward whomever is most known, active, and visible in the acquisition market, and it may not be the best choice for them. If you were to do a few acquisitions in a market (as we did), you will probably get multiple calls from people who are ready to talk — even those you have never approached.

To establish your identity as a great option for potential sellers, you will engage in a process that is very similar to targeting agents you might want to recruit, or even an agent beginning to service a particular market area.

Market MLS reports on company and office production are a great way to begin creating a list by comparing historical production with real-time activity. They readily provide average sales price, current inventory, and individual agent production, all of which you can compare to prior quarters or years.

You may find companies that have had a great reputation in the past living off their reputation as the production slides. Companies you did not feel were approachable may surface. It is a matter of getting the word out to the market in a variety of ways; in effect, you are planting seeds everywhere, which may eventually bear fruit with an acquisition.

Below is a sample search for potential candidates from a local market.

MLS Research Last Twelve Months Company Name	Closed Sales Vol.	% of Total	Sold Avg (1000's)	Sold Units	% of Total	Active Vol (1000's)	% of Total	Active Avg (1000's)	Active Units	% of Total
MLS Total	20,522,548		601	34,171		4,386,630		737	5,950	
Zebra Realty	1,906,128	9.3%	1,282	1,487	4.4%	395,615	9.0%	2,018	196	3.3%
Sun Realty	1,405,148	6.9%	1,011	1,390	4.1%	197,572	4.5%	1,074	184	3.1%
Hawkins Realty	898,505	4.4%	1,030	872	2.6%	226,324	5.2%	1,741	130	2.2%
Wilson Realty	864,135	4.2%	1,245	694	2.0%	267,726	6.1%	2,159	124	2.1%
Mountain Living	741,284	3.6%	333	2,224	6.5%	226,027	5.2%	616	367	6.2%

Tracking Candidates

We suggest that once you get down to your list of candidates (this list could be 2 or 20 companies long) to begin tracking the targets.

Make it a manageable job by doing the detailed work on your prime candidates. Go back one year to start and look at the monthly trends for each of the companies over that period. Track as much information as possible, including (but not limited to):

- Sales price
- Listing inventory
- Days on market
- List to sale ratio

- Listing price to selling price ratio
- Closed sales
- Pending sales
- Individual agent production
- Agent churn

We have even worked with firms that will map where in the market the listings and sales occurred. The adventurous even map the agent's homes, if that information is available.

Yes, this is all pre-work to identify and know as much (or more) about these companies than the owners do. This should provide insight into a company that may be struggling or those that are really doing well. When it comes time for your meetings, at the appropriate time, you can say " I see that your sales are up X % in the last four months, or that your listing inventory has declined over last year by X%."

Even if you do not ever acquire any of these companies, this should give you a competitive edge with unmatched knowledge of the market and a deeper understanding of what your competitors are doing to generate their business and where.

We always recommend, even before contacting another firm, that you have completed your internal assessment and preliminary research. Once done, you should be able to compare your internal SWOT analysis and needs with an estimate of the potential candidate.

The following is the SWOT competitor analysis concept that we use. This should be modified as needed for your individual requirements in your market.

ACQUIRING MORE PROFIT

SWOT COMPETITOR ANALYSIS
(Qualitative and Quantitative)

Competitive Index - 202X

Comparisons	Ofc Locations	Agents	Sales Vol.	Listings	Est. GCI	Other
Your Firm						
Firm A						
Firm B						
Firm C						
Firm D						

Internal Factors

Comparisons	Ofc Locations	Agents	Sales Vol.	Listings	Est. GCI	Other
STRENGTHS	Your Firm	Firm A	Firm B	Firm C	Firm D	
Value Prop						
Agents						
Management						
Brand						
Advantages						

Comparisons	Ofc Locations	Agents	Sales Vol.	Listings	Est. GCI	Other
WEAKNESSES						
Sales Decline						
Agent Loss						
Price Point						
Other						
Improvements						

External Factors

Comparisons	Ofc Locations	Agents	Sales Vol.	Listings	Est. GCI	Other
OPPORTUNITIES	Your Firm	Firm A	Firm B	Firm C	Firm D	
Market						
Location						
Recruiting						
Favorable Trends						

Comparisons	Ofc Locations	Agents	Sales Vol.	Listings	Est. GCI	Other
THREATS	Your Firm	Firm A	Firm B	Firm C	Firm D	
Obstacles						
Economic Climate						
Market Shifts						
Vulnerabilities						

We like this version of the SWOT approach because it contains a qualitative narrative that requires self-reflection around where you rank compared to your competitors. By combining this narrative with a quantitative assessment based on actual data points in one form, it should lead you to a very accurate indication of your rank.

When performed annually, it can become the foundation of your business plan and can give you a realistic assessment of what your competitors have done right or wrong during the past year compared to your company.

This template is available in the Implementation Guide so that you can easily add categories and competitors based on your firm's needs.

Chapter 3: Approaching a Candidate

We are making progress! By now, you have compiled a list of potential candidates, done your initial diligence, and you are now ready for what might be the most difficult part of the process: approaching a candidate.

Unfortunately, we have worked with a number of companies (which shall remain nameless) that were great at the internal assessment, identifying candidates, and the research component. They spent months, if not years, preparing for an M&A deal with wonderful, deep information.

Here's what sometimes happens next: They put the analysis aside and say, "I'll get back to this acquisition stuff later, when I have more time." Before you know it, six months have gone by, and before they can consider their M&A options in the marketplace, they have to start the research over again. They never did get the nerve to talk with their prime candidates, and so the process stopped.

Analysis is necessary, of course — but remember that no acquisition we ever worked on was *ever* completed without an initial contact of some sort. Any delay in making the contact with a company you've identified as a quality prospect could result in a competitor — possibly one who has done no research or made no preparation — calling the candidate and beginning the process before you take the opportunity.

Some people are not good cold-callers. We understand and empathize if this describes you; we are not great at it, either! Reaching out to a candidate is simple to do, but it is not always easy. For many, it is an activity that lies far outside their comfort zone.

Instead of a cold call, we believe the initial contact should be a "warm call." Hopefully, the person you're reaching out to will be someone you have met at an industry event, or at least acquainted with someone you know. Networking and connections do help with the initial call.

If you don't know any brokers in the market, don't panic. Maybe it is a new one for you. We have worked in many new markets where we do not know any brokers. Most are willing take a meeting with us because they are curious about what we are up to in the market.

Once we talk with one broker in the market (and assume for this discussion they are not interested), then we ask them who else in the market is a good competitor, and someone they respect. We usually already know the brokers they recommend, but it's always a good idea to ask.

We can now go to those brokers, and when they ask why we are approaching them, we can tell them they have been mentioned by their peers as a quality broker and competitor in the local market. We do not use the referring broker's name unless given permission, but this usually sets the broker's mind at ease that it is not (entirely) a cold call and that we are seriously in the market looking to expand.

It is important not to rush things too much as you get to this stage. Starting an acquisition is exciting, but if you are too anxious or aggressive in your initial approach to a candidate, you can easily cause them to not engage or scare them off.

Your goal is to build a pipeline of potential candidates for today, but also in the future. That is why your initial conversation with a candidate should not include words like "takeover," "buyout," "absorb," "close down" — all phrases we have heard — or anything along those lines. You have to build a trusting relationship slowly, and the first contact may very well be your most important one.

Hoby Hanna of Hanna Holdings is quick to point out that a competitor will rarely admit that they want to sell. As we all know, a rumor of a sale in real estate can be harmful to agent recruiting and retention.

Hanna notes that the conversation should always center around synergies and operational benefits as well as financial and succession planning. As we'll discuss further, when you approach the opportunity, it is critical that the buyer and the seller both sit on the same side of the table and work together toward a mutually beneficial outcome.

Finding The Right Approach

We travel on airplanes frequently, and being bored, often flip through the airline's sponsored magazine in the seat pocket. Inevitably, there is a full-page ad for the dating service It's Just Lunch.

Presumably, this dating service is successful with professionals because everyone has to eat; they may waste an hour or so of their lives, but it was an hour they'd spend eating, anyway, and the potential for finding a partner for life could be great. (Dear wives: We have never used this service and never intend to.)

This concept applies very well to the acquisition process. Your first contact is really similar to a first date. You want it to be non-threatening, to take place in a neutral environment, and to just get together to learn more about each other and your businesses. The worst that can happen out of it is they get a free lunch, breakfast, or coffee, and they learn a little more about an industry competitor. The best-case scenario is that you could both find a long-term opportunity that would be beneficial and profitable to everyone.

As you establish contact with a candidate, the approach and the tone that you adopt will set the stage for future conversations. We will examine a number of different approaches.

There are instances in which you may choose a more "direct" approach, which might be appropriate in a situation in which you need to move ahead quickly (such as with a struggling company). Or you may opt for more of a "soft sell" approach when dealing with a more successful candidate, who may never have considered selling or are simply not ready to sell their company —yet.

Third-Party Approach

We (and others) have also been hired in the past to conduct everything from researching potential markets, possible candidates, and the entire M&A process. If you are not comfortable with the process, you have limited time, or this is not your strength, you could easily outsource the research and initial contacts at a minimum.

This approach often works best when wanting to merge with or acquire a company in a completely new market. At some point after the candidate's interest is qualified by a third party, you will need to be involved to establish the rapport and trust required for a successful outcome.

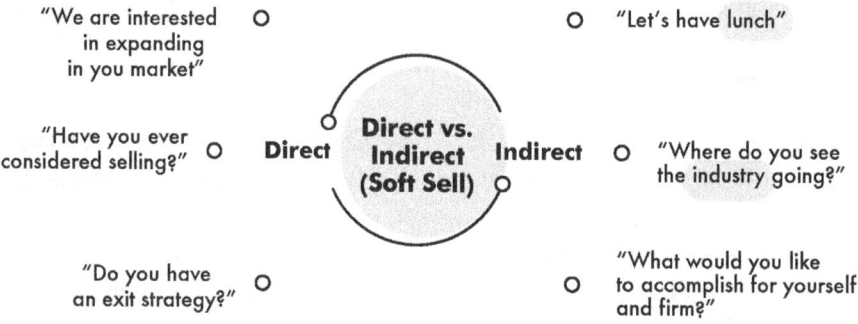

Sample First Calls

When beginning your actual meetings, we have always felt it is a good idea to practice your approach first on a few candidates that you feel may not be prime. Save your preferred or ideal candidates for after you have been able to adjust your presentation and feel comfortable with it.

The purpose with all of the approaches is to get to a first meeting and to leave a good first impression. You do not have to be perfect, but ideally you can communicate sincerity, humility, and position yourself as a potential "great future partner" in all communications.

Everyone has their own particular conversational style, and it is best to be as natural as possible when first talking with a candidate. Of course, much will be dictated by how well you know the person, your relationship, and how any previous conversations have unfolded.

If you follow a rehearsed script too closely, the call may end up sounding like a canned pitch that you have tried on a dozen other brokers. Still, it is useful to practice your pitch and even use bullet points or an outline to feel comfortable.

As you know, you only get one chance to make a first impression, and you want to be on your A-Game. Below are some sample phone approaches, with variations that should be adapted to your preferred approach. These are listed in descending order from most to least direct.

1. *Good morning, Sally, this is John at ABC Realty. Is this a good time to talk?....(insert some nice chit chat)....Sally, I'm not sure if you've heard, but we are aggressively expanding our company. I know you have built a fine company and have an outstanding reputation, and I was wondering if you had ever considered selling? I would like to tell you more about what we are up to and hear a little more about your own future plans. Could I meet you for a coffee in the next couple of weeks?*

2. *Good morning, Sally, this is John at ABC Realty...(insert some nice chit-chat).... Sally, we are going to be expanding in your area soon. In our research, we saw that you and your company are one of the finest and most respected in the market. We are currently looking for a quality partner that would be interested in joining forces with us to maximize their growth potential. I would very much like to buy you lunch so we can share what we are up to in your market, find out about your future plans, and discuss how we might be able to mutually benefit each other. At the very least, I would like to meet you as I have heard so many good things about you.*

3. *Good morning Sally, This is John at ABC Realty. I am interested in growing my company, and I have always admired you and your firm. I am wondering if there may be a way that we could bring our firms together in some manner that would be beneficial to us both. I am not sure what that looks like, but I would very much like to share my*

thoughts and explore the opportunity. Do you have any time available in the next week to meet?

4. *Good morning Sally, This is John at ABC Realty. I was hoping we might meet for lunch in the near future. I am interested in learning your views on where the real estate market is going in the next few years, and I would be happy to share with you what I am thinking in exchange, and where we would like to go with our company.*

Notice that none of these overtures are very specific. The sole purpose of the call is to set up a casual meeting over breakfast, lunch, or a coffee.

Generally, you will not get turned down when you make such a simple request. Most real estate people love to talk about the business and learn a little bit more about their competitors. When pressed, they may say, "if this is about buying me out, I am not interested."

A good response is as follows: "This is about learning a little more about each other, and all options are on the table." You could discuss anything from working on some programs or training together, to a joint venture of a new office or market, to a merger, or even you selling your own company.

We have often advised that you really don't know going into every opportunity if you are the buyer, potential merger partner, or even the seller. We try not to rule anything out.

Persistence Pays Off

A lot of people may be taken aback when you first call; you are catching them "off guard," and they are not sure what you are really up to, and that could be the reason behind any trepidation. This can be especially true if you do not have a prior relationship with them.

We like offering to them something like the following: "At the very least, you'll know a little bit more about my company, and I'll know a little bit more about yours, and maybe we can do more business together in the future."

If you cannot convince someone to meet with you, then at that point, you should be friendly and courteous and say: "Well, maybe we can get together in a couple of months." And then put it in your calendar, and call them back again in six to eight weeks.

During those two months, a lot of changes can occur. Always treat a "no" as a "not now." In our dealings with potential candidates, we have had people say "no" for two years — then all of a sudden, we call and they respond with "I am glad you called." Timing and persistence are keys to creating a sustainable and a successful acquisition strategy.

Some brokers prefer to make connections outside of the telephone. Another strategy we have seen that has worked is attending events that will facilitate conversations between brokers. Future M&A meetings often start by being in the same room as a candidate or seated next to them at a table. You can then gradually introduce a "working more together" conversation and propose getting together for lunch in the future.

If you prefer to avoid the phone approach, there are many opportunities in our industry and within our communities to get together with a potential candidate for a two-minute conversation. Again, keep the same goal in mind: to secure a private meeting in the future.

The First Meeting

Whether it's achieved through a cold-call, direct mail, or through a bit of cocktail party maneuvering, the end result of your initial contact should be to have a meeting set up.

Who should be at that first meeting? It depends. If there are a couple of partners involved at the other company, you might start out talking to one and bring the other partner or partners in later.

You do *not* want this to be a presentation. We have found we prefer to talk with one partner, get them on our side, and let them assist with the process.

Sometimes you must meet with everyone. On the positive side, if there are three partners or more, there is a pretty good chance that at least one of them may want to get out of the situation.

With regard to spouses or significant others, it is preferable to have only the principal at the first meeting or two — though you will want to involve any partners and family before too long, as we will discuss later.

In setting up that first meeting, you will need to:

- Determine the participants
- Choose an appropriate and convenient time
- Choose a neutral venue
- Do as much homework on the person and company as possible

The meeting should be held at a neutral site — a restaurant or coffee shop are both good choices.

It can also be a good idea to hold the meeting somewhere outside the market area. You will have to determine your market and what people would surmise from seeing the two of you talking together alone.

Of course, your conversation could be about Board business, a conference, a community event you are both involved in, or just friendly intel-gathering. Our suggestion is to act like you're just getting to know the person across the table if someone sees you or even approaches you.

Remember: It is always appropriate to talk and learn about real estate from a competitor. But you should do everything possible to help keep both potential buyers' and potential sellers' reputations intact and minimize rumor-mongering.

Confidentiality Is Critical

Your goal is to make the potential seller as comfortable as possible with the discussions and the process. They will be looking for reasons not to proceed more than reasons to go forward with the discussions.

Most would-be sellers are very afraid (with good reason) of their agents or the market finding out about serious discussions about selling. At some point — usually during the second or third meeting — you and the seller should both sign a non-disclosure agreement (NDA), which is sometimes called a confidentiality agreement.

These documents are typically signed after both parties agree to explore M&A possibilities through further discussions. The agreement states that all information exchanged and learned in ensuing conversations from non-public sources will be kept in confidence for a certain number of years, specified and documented in the agreement.

In addition to you, any person in your company or family who knows about these conversations, should understand the critical importance of maintaining absolute confidentiality during the acquisition.

This is a serious matter. If the information leaks (especially from your side), it could not only cause the loss of trust and the end of this transaction for you, but also a loss of agents for the seller. And that's not all: A leak could damage any future attempts to talk to other brokers in the community because they will be worried that you cannot maintain confidentiality.

We have always used and recommend that you use a code word for the person or firm's name you are meeting with. An example is assigning the project a code name of "Hawk" if the seller happens to be an Atlanta Hawks basketball fan, or even just if the firm is in Atlanta. We would put "Hawk" in all meeting appointments, emails, and information exchanges internally.

This is especially useful if others not privy to the discussions are exposed to the information, even inadvertently. Bottom line: You do not want a leak to come from your side.

Unfortunately, in our experience, *both* sides must be prepared for the word to get out even as they take steps to prevent leaks. This usually happens late in the process, and it's usually a result of the seller not being quite as careful as they should be. It's better to discuss the possibility upfront and come up with a plan for how each should react before it happens.

Our advice is that a seller should always be looking for ways to improve their company, and they will listen to and entertain all manner of opportunities. It is the broker's job to find the best options for their company and agents. The agents need to trust that they will make the right choice to proceed with any improvements and inform everyone when appropriate.

A number of days before Pacific Union closed on the sale to Compass, Inman News broke the story. Neither company could comment on the story, and it put Pacific Union's CEO, Mark McLaughlin — and the office managers — in a difficult position with the agents.

Exploring The Future

As we discussed in an earlier chapter, it's vital to know as much as you can about the company and person before you meet. Through your knowledge of their company, you can show the potential candidate that this is more than just a casual meeting; you have taken a genuine interest in their company. This should be flattering to them and also tells them that you have two things they might want in their company: quality management skills and your finger on the pulse of the market.

There are five major objectives for the first meeting (and it may take two or three meetings to cover all of them):

1. To get to know the person and the company better, and they you
2. To give the impression that you are a competent and trusted leader
3. Get the candidate interested enough to consider a second meeting
4. Nudge the candidate to contemplate that they may have a better option than owning a real estate company currently
5. Begin to uncover the potential motivation for selling and the deal's timing

We always like to begin the meeting by finding out more about their family and outside interests, letting them know the non-real estate life side is as important to you as the business side. Sometimes it is best for you to start telling them about *your* business and personal life. We always like to hear the story of how someone ended up in the real estate business and owning a company.

You will eventually transition to the topic of where you are as a company and where you hope to take your business. We feel it is fine to discuss struggles you may have had (the market probably knows all about them), but it's more important to share (selectively) how you overcame those hurdles. The challenges you share could be financial, personal, loss of agents, and so on.

It's better to get that topic out of the way early; this is an opportunity to show humility in addition to confidence in the future and your vision for where you're going. This is not the time to boast, but self-assurance is welcome. Remember to treat this as an interview for the opportunity to lead this person and their agents into the future.

This process will hopefully coax the candidate to talk about their own hopes, dreams, and challenges in the real estate business. This is precisely where you want to lead the conversation.

If the conversation begins veering toward a sale, often one of the first questions a potential candidate will ask is "how much would you pay me?" So how do you respond?

In the first few meetings, you really have no idea what the offer will be and cannot even make an educated guess. If pressed, we will answer by explaining the process and sharing how we would derive the price by mutually agreeing on the adjusted earnings.

Often, these pricing conversations will lean toward multiples of revenue or earnings. Sometimes it is a price per agent. If the seller asks these questions, avoid giving a solid answer. Too often, the averages that are calculated after a sale can mislead the valuation. It is not uncommon to see a company sell for 3X EBITDA (earnings before interest, taxes, depreciation, and amortization) in the same market where another sold for 13X. The purchase price is the exact amount that a buyer will pay and the seller is willing to accept.

Securing An Agreement To Engage

When the appropriate time in the conversation comes, you have to engage them to even agree to consider an opportunity. This may happen during the first meeting, or it could take several.

We usually say something like:

"This is a discovery process for us both, and you are welcome to stop at any time; it will take some effort to fully explore the opportunity. I do not in any way want to waste your time. Please know that I am very serious, but first we need to determine if we can work together successfully.

Let me ask: Would joining forces <u>be the right decision for you, your family, and your agents?</u> (This is a key phrase.) We will begin by spending some time together, exchanging ideas, and exploring where you and your firm want to go.

I want to learn as much as I can about you and your firm. I want you to learn about me, our offering, and my team. We should make sure that our real estate philosophy and goals are aligned. Whether we decide to move forward or not, this is a big decision for us both, and I will proceed at a pace you are comfortable with. At a minimum, we part as friends, and you find out how someone else views the value of your firm. How does this sound?

We like to refer to this as "engaging in the process." It is usually easier for the seller to understand that this is a process they control and that they can exit at any time. The goal for you is to lead to a conclusion one way or the other in a methodical fashion, always moving forward (which is easier said than done sometimes).

The process should be presented as beneficial to the seller even if it never leads to a transaction with you — because it is. They will learn more about their own company, get insight into a competitor's business, and take a look at their firm's perceived valuation.

Finding and Solving The Problem

How are you going to help the seller — either personally or professionally, or both?

It is imperative in the process to find a problem to solve so that the seller sees the value of your offering.

For example: What will the seller do next in their life and career? The problem could be that owning their existing company is holding them back from their next big life shift. The opportunity is for you to help them get to their next chapter as quickly and easily as possible.

1. Find the problem.
2. Determine the motivation.
3. Solve the problem(s) with an opportunity.
4. Become the best, most desirable option.

Our favorite question to uncover the problem to solve is the following: If you were not the owner of your company, what would you be doing instead?

How would you answer? There are only four large buckets of answers that we have encountered:

1. I made more money as an agent; I would be doing personal production. (This response is very common; your best agent ever can frequently be a former owner who knows exactly how hard your job is and is relieved that you are doing it, not them).
2. I would like to retire — to Florida, Alaska, to sail around the world. Alternatives: I would like to retire in a few years, or "soon."
3. I would like to be doing a different job, potentially in an entirely different profession — such as real estate sales training, or ministry, charity work, health care, law, higher education, and so on.
4. I really don't know; I have never thought about it before.

These are the only four answers that we've heard, and we have gotten them in all their variations many times. Even if the seller does not know, or they are not ready to answer, this question will definitely get them thinking. At the next meeting, they may have an answer.

If they say they do not know, a good follow-up question is: If we asked your spouse, significant other, or family what you would or should be doing instead, what would *they* say?

Often, the person will say, "My spouse has wanted me to retire for a few years," or "My family saw more of me and I made more money when I was in personal production," or "My significant other would like to travel more, and I have been promising we would."

Their answer tells you what they might want to do with their next chapter. It could be a definite — they are ready — or a dream they hope to fulfill. You can be the one to help them get there. You have now gotten them thinking there may be a viable path to what they really would prefer doing rather than owning a real estate company.

This discovery will be the motivation for selling. Remember, the reason they're even thinking about selling is probably because they are not making enough money for the time invested, and so a sale might be a good move for them. This information also builds a strong foundation for a relationship and the ability to work toward the goal together. You are demonstrating that you will assist, not only financially side but also by showing them that the next chapter in their life is attainable — and you can be the one to help them get there.

Remember that there is a difference between the reason for selling (which is usually financial) and the motivation that will cause them to sell. What you will need to discover is the motivation that would cause them to sell the firm at this time, and more importantly, sell it to you.

If the seller is a small broker who is still in personal production, it is very likely that they will earn more as a sales person than a broker-owner. When Byron Grant sold South County Realty to Century 21 Hometown Realty, this is exactly what happened. Grant focused on what he did best, had more personal time, and made more money with less risk.

Don't forget death and divorce. These events might also trigger the interest in selling as these events have significant estate planning ramifications.

Exit Strategy

Often, we have used the approach of asking a potential target, "What is your exit strategy"?

Most real estate owners have not thought about one, and therefore they do not have a formal strategy in place they are executing. An exit strategy is a relatively simple concept, but it requires deep thinking and planning around how and when a business owner will divest their ownership in the company. The goal of a strong exit strategy is to maximize the value of the company and realize a return on investment while also minimizing risk and uncertainty.

You as a buyer may be part of the exit plan, or perhaps you are competing against their other options for their future. There are several different types of exit strategies that a business owner may consider, including:

1. **Selling the company to another business or individual, either internal or external.** This can be a good option if the company has a strong market position, solid earnings, and there are potential buyers interested in acquiring it.
2. **Going public.** This is only an option for the really large real estate firms, which involves issuing shares of the company's stock on a public exchange, such as the NYSE or NASDAQ.
3. **Merging with another company.** This involves combining the operations of two companies into a single entity. This can be a good option for companies that are looking to expand their market presence or gain access to new technologies, complementary management, or additional resources.
4. **Liquidating the company.** This involves selling off the company's assets and closing the doors. Every year, there are still a number of firms that just close down. They may not know there is another method, or that their firm has value, or an estate or an heir makes

the decision. This is typically considered as a last resort and is usually only pursued if the company is unable to continue operating or if there are no other viable exit options.

Exploring The Future

Finding out what the seller wants to do after the sale may require many conversations and some input and suggestions on your part. You'll need to build trust before most people feel comfortable really opening up to you and sharing their dreams and hopes. (We have also worked with sellers who were "open books" on the first meeting; everyone is unique.)

You may have to help the process along, probing the person's strengths and weaknesses, the things they like and don't like about the business. It may be as simple as asking, "What do you enjoy most about running your own office?"…and, "What drives you crazy about it?"

It is important to get the seller to think hypothetically, to move beyond the here-and-now and begin to consider the realm of possibilities. What if they were not bogged down by financial struggles or day-to-day administrative duties — what could they be doing with their time if they were given freedom from existing restraints?

What you will discover, more often than not, is that the seller would like to escape the day-to-day challenges that an owner typically faces. In many cases, owners never really wanted to take on all these headaches in the first place.

Many successful agents just naturally progress toward owning their own business. We all know that the most successful salespeople do not always make the best managers. It is an entirely different skill set that must be learned and nurtured.

Once they are owners, they may discover that they really do not enjoy recruiting, training, motivating, and being responsible for everyone else's problems. On top of that, they are probably earning less money with more hassle than they did in personal production. They may have realized by now (or with your help) that they really just love to sell, or train agents, work on marketing programs, or even be a sales manager.

Play To Their Strengths

If you can identify where an owner's strengths and passion lie (hopefully still real-estate-related), then you have a great opportunity to help them create a "second career" within your company and most likely strengthen your company in the process.

Some broker-owners are excellent at doctoring deals; others are great at marketing or have a passion for technology. Finding a role in the company that allows the seller to concentrate on their superpower will often result in wider success for everyone.

When John Coile sold Champion Real Estate to Berkshire Hathaway Home Services of America, he found a passion for representing the firm's industry relationships with the National Association of REALTORS and MLS Policy — roles that he would not have had time to develop as an owner-operator.

Indeed, the seller may be one of the greatest single assets of the company you are acquiring. Keep in mind that people who have run their own company are probably the best agents or employees that you could hope to find. They are generally more loyal; many agents suspect the owners are pocketing exorbitant amounts of profits and not doing much work, but a former owner understands the thin margins and the resources and work required to be successful. Because they have been on both sides, as both an owner and employee (or agent), they can often serve as a calming influence and liaison with your staff and agents. Former owners can be particularly helpful in maintaining stability in the critical first 90 days of a transaction.

Roles The Seller Might Play Within Your Company Post-M&A

1. Senior Sales Agent

2. Branch Manager/Sales Manager

3. COO/CFO

4. Recruiting Director

5. Property Manager/Commercial Manager

6. Referral Director

7. New Homes Director

8. Training Director

9. Contracts/Compliance Manager

10. Advisory Board Member/ VP of X

11. Marketing Director

12. Technology Director

Saving Face

If someone is selling you their business, they want to make a change in how they're spending their time every day. You can help the seller find a role and title that suits their talent so they feel good about themselves and their decision.

We never suggest offering a person the wrong role, but through the discovery process, you will find an area they are good at and enjoy, and you can use that to craft a potential future for them that appeals to each individual seller. Remember: Is the seller making a business decision or an emotional one? The answer is *yes* ... to both questions.

Selling a firm is often a very emotional decision. Many broker-owners have invested their life's work, thousands of hours, and their savings into the firm, or it might have even been passed down a generation or two. Sellers want to know they have done the best thing for themselves, their legacy, their employees, and their agents. Although money is always important, rarely is a sale only about the money.

Many people feel they cannot sell the company for $X because of the factors mentioned above. The amount you may offer looks small compared to everything that they have put into building and growing their firm, even if it has not been a financial success. They look at the personal investment and sacrifices made — not the opportunity cost of not selling now, of continuing to defer dreams, and not being able to do what they would rather be doing sooner.

You must help convince them that their accomplishments in building their company is the springboard to their future. Without all they have invested to date, they would not have the opportunity to move to their next chapter. They have not failed in any way!

Most people crave to be perceived as a success: to themselves, to their community and their family. Your job is to help them feel good about the M&A process, about themselves, and about selling to you. Give them the ability to tell all: "I could not resist merging with them; we received a very generous price (too good to pass up); it is a great opportunity for my staff and agents, and I now have the ability to do what I have wanted to do for a long time."

This emotional transition to feeling good about selling is the tipping point to a successful transaction. Your ability to show them a new opportunity, whatever it may be, is the significant advantage you have over the pure financial transactions that national, regional, and most local buyers (at least those who have not read this book) employ.

It is also critical that the seller does not poison the well. Clearly there will be operational changes after the transaction that will require adjustment. The seller is not likely to approve of every change, but it is vital that they understand that any action that undermines the changes that are happening at the company with agents, staff, or managers will be detrimental to the success of the transaction.

The Win-Win Philosophy of Negotiating

In the first *Acquiring Profit* book, I covered the win-win approach to conducting mergers and acquisitions. Many still believe there is always one winner and one loser in any negotiation. We feel that in an acquisition that is conducted on solid terms, especially with an earn-out provision, there is a powerful motivator for both sides to work together in the process.

This "working together relationship" closely resembles a partnership or joint venture and extends beyond the closing; we believe it is the best approach to maximize the benefits for both the buyer and seller.

Groundbreaking research was done in the field of negotiation many years ago (and still applies today) by Dr. Stephen Covey, author of the best-selling book *The 7 Habits of Highly Effective People*, as well as Roger Fisher and William Ury, who taught negotiation at Harvard University for many years.

According to Covey, "Most people tend to think in terms of dichotomies: strong or weak, hardball or softball, win or lose. But that kind of thinking is fundamentally flawed." As Covey notes, most business people are living in an "interdependent reality" — meaning that the people they deal with will continue to have some impact on them, even after a particular deal is finished.

In a win-lose situation, Covey points out, the loser may not fulfill the contract, they may carry grudges and battle scars into future dealings with you, and they may spread that negative attitude to others. "In the long run, if it isn't a win for both of us," says Covey, "then we both lose."

Fisher and Ury, in their best-selling book *Getting To Yes*, echo that philosophy. According to Fisher and Ury, "in most instances, to ask a negotiator who's winning is as inappropriate as to ask who's winning a marriage."

Instead, they advocate what is known as "principled negotiations" — in which negotiators focus on shared interests rather than opposing positions, and in which the two parties try to create options that will benefit everyone.

We contend that the win-win philosophy is ideally suited to the real estate business, specifically the buying and selling of firms, where so much is dependent on human interactions and long- term relationships. After the transaction closes, both the buyer and the seller need the acquired agents to be as productive and content as possible.

The buyer needs the seller to be supportive and let them know if there have been any issues that have arisen, even after a couple of years, to maximize their revenue. The seller needs the buyer to lead their agents and make them as productive as possible to maximize the earn-out. Without both working together and in unison, neither will be able to achieve the full benefit of the transaction.

Changing Attitudes

In some ways, it may be difficult for people engaging in real estate acquisitions to accept the win-win philosophy; after all, this is an extremely competitive and ego-driven business, and many people in real estate tend to have a "beat-your-competitor-at-any cost" syndrome. Shareholders or Board Members who demand every cent of profit to be squeezed from an acquisition may be just looking at the spreadsheets. However, we believe that once you begin the acquisition process, this person is no longer the enemy — now they are your potential future partner. This is the engagement philosophy that hopefully leads to a long and successful marriage.

Relationship-building is not always quick or easy, as we'll cover in the next chapter. It takes time, effort, flexibility, and a willingness to look at everything from the other person's point of view.

Chapter 4: Relationship-Building

The concept of relationship-building is central to one's success in real estate acquisitions. Your ability to develop a rapport with the seller based on mutual trust and respect is more than just a matter of goodwill; in the end, it can have a significant impact, either positive or negative, on the price you pay for the company. It could even affect whether or not the seller will seriously contemplate a transaction with you.

Moreover, your success or failure in cultivating a positive relationship with the seller is likely to continue to have repercussions long after the acquisition is completed.

Why is this true? It relates directly to the particular nature of the real estate business. When an owner sells a firm, they aren't just selling "bricks and mortar." They often feel as if they are selling part of themselves. For that reason, they want to sell to someone they can be proud to be associated with and someone they can trust.

With rare exceptions, we have found that owners truly care about their employees and the agents who are part of their company; they also care about their reputation in the community. In most transactions we have seen fail, the buyer has a "customer" mentality, similar to buying a boat or car. The thought is that you are doing the salesman or dealer a favor by taking the boat or car off their hands.

Most successful acquisitions involve people who like each other and respect each other. Both parties have appreciation for the personal and business aspects of the relationship, which is dramatically different than a customer approach. We have worked for a number of national firms that had a customer approach, combined with a win-lose attitude. This does not and did not bode well for the relationship post-closing, and many times the earnings for both sides suffered.

Sellers all go through five significant decision phases before a transaction is consummated. Your job is to help them through each phase and understand that they cannot skip any; it may take hours, days, or years to move through each one.

The Five Phases of a Seller's Decisions

1. They must decide *whether* they want to sell

2. They must decide *when* they want to sell

3. They must decide *what they will do next* with their career and life

4. They must accept a *price* that someone is willing to pay

5. They must decide whether *you are the right partner*

Seller's Decision Process

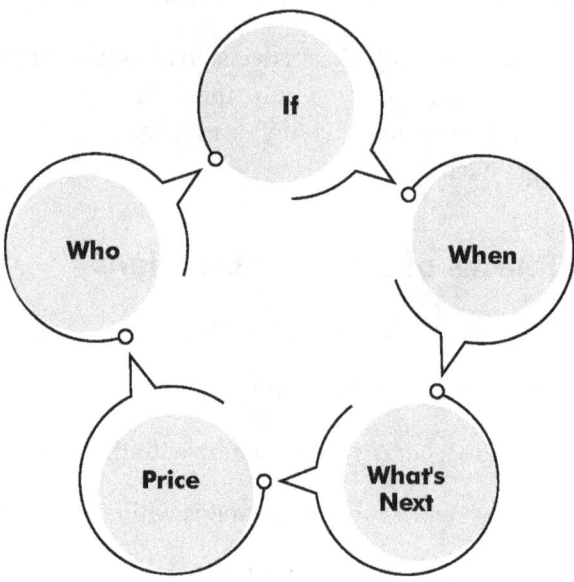

The above decision tree emphasizes why we believe relationship-building and trust are the critical elements to a successful transaction. Every seller goes through the same steps, and they often need guidance along the way.

Popular Reasons Why Brokers Want To Sell

There are a variety of reasons why a brokerage owner might decide to sell their business. Some common reasons include:

1. **Retirement:** Many firm-owners start their businesses later in life and decide to sell their company when they are ready to retire.
2. **Personal health issues:** An owner may decide to sell their business if they are unable to continue operating it due to personal health issues.

3. **Lack of interest:** An owner may lose interest in the business and decide to sell it to focus on other interests or pursuits.

4. **Financial pressures:** An owner may choose to sell their business if they are experiencing financial pressures that make it difficult to continue operating the business.

5. **Opportunity to sell at a profit:** An owner may decide to sell their business if they believe they can sell it for a profit and use the proceeds to pursue other opportunities.

6. **Lack of succession plan:** An owner may not have a plan for transferring ownership of the business to a family member or employee, and may decide to sell the business instead.

7. **Lack of resources:** An owner may decide to sell their business if they do not have the resources or expertise to take the business to the next level.

Overall, there are many factors that can influence an owner's decision to sell their business, and each individual's circumstances will be unique.

Trust Equals Value

This may be the most critical equation in a successful M&A transaction.

If a seller is convinced that you, the buyer, can be trusted to take care of their people, their good name, and their lifetime investment — and that you might even help the agents become more productive — that can translate to real value to the seller. If they feel you are the one to maximize their earn-out, and ultimately the total amount they receive for the firm, then you may be able to secure the acquisition for a lower price than a less-trustworthy offer.

The reverse is true as well. If the seller is selling reluctantly, and they do not have faith in your ability to retain and lead the agents, that will put you in a weaker position as a buyer.

If you are perceived by the seller this way, that does not mean you cannot acquire another company, but you will invariably pay more upfront and may even be priced out of the transaction.

Building a strong relationship with the seller has other ramifications beyond impacting the price. It can influence the future success of the transaction, as it may determine whether the seller and other key players in their company will work with you or against you once the transaction is completed.

Empathy Is The Key

How, exactly, do you build a strong relationship with a seller? It really begins with empathy — the ability to put yourself in someone else's shoes and consider their needs.

As stated by Fisher and Ury, this is a somewhat radical concept in the world of negotiations because so many assume that negotiations are all about winning and "looking out for number one." But the fact is that if you are going to be successful at relationship-building, you will have to look at every step in the process from all viewpoints.

Immediate And Long-Term Needs

While determining the future role of the seller in your company is one of the key aspects of building a relationship, there are other needs of the seller which should be addressed.

In general, the seller's needs can be separated into two categories, long-term and short-term. The long-term needs relate to career and future. If they have not saved enough for retirement, for example, these needs raise the questions, "How am I going to get back into a productive and profitable lifestyle, pay for my children's college, pay off the house, buy that second home" — or even, "How am I going to afford a new car?" Satisfying long-term needs usually involves finding a way for the seller to make a living and enjoy the rest of their career.

Often in the sale of a real estate company, there are more "immediate needs," which tend to be more pressing in nature. Immediate needs usually involve some sort of debt. There may be business bills that have piled up, or a credit line, lease buyout, or loan balloon due shortly. Those debts may also be tied in with personal financial problems at home, or simply cash-flow shortfalls. For the seller, these immediate needs raise the questions, "How am I going to make it to next month — the heck with next year?!"

Debt and cash-flow issues are not necessarily bad when purchasing a company. They could have occurred outside of the seller's control — for example, medical problems might have played a role — or because they are not good money managers. Financial issues are important to discover quickly, but by themselves, these should not be deal-stoppers.

If the company is sound from a top-line perspective and you know you can manage the expense portion better, this is an opportunity to provide options and solutions. You have uncovered the primary motivation for the seller, and if you can solve the problem, it could be a huge win for you both.

Most buyers will say, "I will give you $X for your company, but it is up to you to deal with a sub-lease of your space, the copier I do not want, the old phone system lease, and all your other agreements." They only want to buy a clean company. This can be a big mistake on the part of a potential buyer.

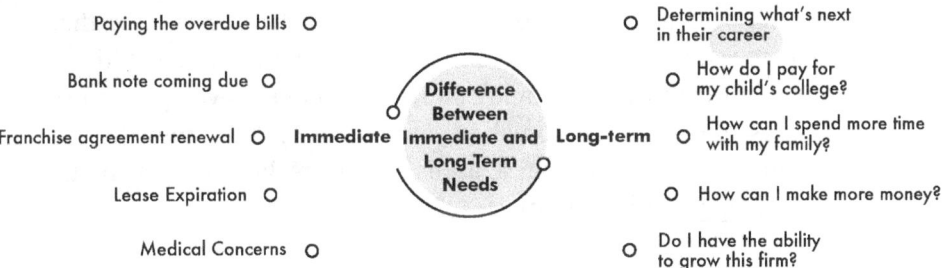

Debts Can Be Opportunities

Debt relief may present a great opportunity for you to help the seller, move the deal forward, and save money in the process.

Often, a seller will think, " I'd like to sell the company, but I can't because I owe too much," or " I do not know how to get out from under these bills." But if you can help solve their financial crunch as part of the sale — by, say, taking over a note obligation, or assisting in restructuring the debt — then this allows the seller to move ahead with the transaction, and more importantly, their life. This gives you a huge advantage over a potential buyer who does not want to deal with any issues other than writing a check.

Naturally, the price you pay for the company would be lowered in relation to the amount of debt you assume, and often you can come out far ahead. The fact is that once a seller has made the decision to sell, they want it to happen with the least amount of hassle to them as possible. They may be so anxious to solve their problems quickly that they are willing to walk away from thousands on the purchase price to relieve their current frustrations.

Keep in mind you are dealing with the seller's various needs, and some may not be evident on the surface. We refer to these as the "underlying needs" of the seller, and they may include everything from debts, to an impending divorce, to problems with the IRS, to agent defections. We have encountered all of these issues and all of them can be worked through to help generate a beneficial transaction to both sides.

These are things that the seller won't necessarily talk about right away. Initially, they're apt to tell you they are tired of the business, or they are ready to retire, or they want to get back into sales. As you cultivate a relationship with the seller and continue to probe, developing trust, these issues (if there are any) will begin to surface. When they do, you should remember not to see these as deal-breakers, but rather a chance for you to help provide solutions.

Considerations To Never Forget

There are some other considerations, which we put under the heading of "Considerations to Never Forget" for a reason: We must confess that over the years, we have at one time or another been burned on every one of these, losing a transaction.

Spouse/significant other.

Topping the list is a dynamic that can turn out to be the wild card in your relationship with the seller.

You may build a great relationship with the seller, agree on a mutually beneficial future and the price and terms. Then the seller conveys this to their spouse or significant other, who becomes outraged — "What do you mean, they are only offering you $500,000?! We must have put $1 million into this business! Are they trying to cheat you?!"

At the root of the problem, often, is the misconception by the partner about the company's true worth and maybe even the current state it is in. They have an inkling that the money has been a little tight lately, but they also have probably been hearing, "the business is just about to turn the corner; everything is going to be fine." If they are not brought into the loop until the end of the negotiation, then it is understandable why they feel your offer might be a low one.

We like to ask early on, "How are decisions made in the company and household?" It is important to get all decision-makers involved in the process, especially ones who share the same home. They can be a huge ally if the relationship is built correctly — or, conversely, your worst nightmare.

Partner or silent partner (investor):

You need to find out early if the person you are dealing with is the decision-maker, one of several, or has no real power to buy or sell. We have found ourselves well down the road in the process with a seller, only to find out there is an investor with significant sway over any decision. In fact, we have had a situation where the investor was a majority owner, and we did not find out until we were finalizing the sale contract!

We can combat that mistake by asking for the ownership percentage and structure early in the diligence process, or by asking "If you were to make a major decision like selling, what is the decision process for approval?"

Employees

Similarly, the employees are usually a critical part of the mix. That is especially true of anyone who's been with the company for a number of years: the administrative person, controller, marketing director, and so on.

Sometimes the staff know more about running the company and what is really going on than the owner does. We have purchased companies where a beloved administrative person was more important to the retention of the agents than the owner. You must make sure you identify the key contributors, consider their future roles, and speak about them respectfully at all times.

Many buyers going into a transaction look for the obvious synergies, saying, "We will not need your controller, we already have a good one — and we have plenty of administrative people, so we will not need yours." Maybe the controller or administrative staff have been there 15 years and are loved by all.

Worse, which has happened to us, the person we talked about letting go immediately was a cousin of the owner! Needless to say, this did not sit well with the seller and caused the negotiations to go sideways.

It's better to keep the staff, at least initially, and factor this consideration into your budget and purchase price. We have seen staff let go, and a week later the buyer's controller gives notice. We have also seen many instances where the seller's staff could be an upgrade over the buyers.

Generally speaking, owners want their employees taken care of. At the announcement, owners want to be able to say to everyone, "I believe the merger of our two fine companies offers a great opportunity for growth for all of our agents and staff." They do not want to go to any staff member and say, "I am sorry; the company has been sold, and there is no need for you at the new company."

Obviously, you do not want to keep duplicate resources ,and we want you to seek synergies; however, we find it best to keep everyone on staff for 90 days until the "dust settles" and you know your needs. You may find some "gem employees" in the seller's company who can be transferred to another branch or the home office. The point remains: We have found talking about getting rid of the seller's employees before you own the company can only get you in trouble.

We have also been involved in a few transactions where one of the employees may get a percentage of the sale, which was given to them as a retention bonus years ago. They typically do not have the ability to kill a deal, but they can definitely create some problems if they feel mis-treated or feel the amount they will receive is not fair. As with all key stakeholders, whether an owner or only an influencer, you want to get them on your side as early as possible.

Sales And/Or Office Managers

As with the employees discussed above, the seller generally wants a good future opportunity for their senior management team. The seller and buyer both need to be able to promote the advantages of the two companies coming together to the management team even before the agents. Throughout an acquisition, if you can remember the phrase: "What is in it for me?", it will serve you well.

The owner is not the only person you should evaluate and spend time with if possible. It is critical that you perform significant diligence to understand who actually has the strongest relationships with the agents.

Do not rely solely on the organizational chart provided or the owner's word. Acknowledging and accounting for the leadership and influence of a general manager, sales or branch manager could be the difference between ultimate success and failure. We have been involved in situations where the seller has overestimated their importance and even their influence on the organization. The agents respected the owner, but they were actually loyal to their immediate manager. The larger the organization, the more likely this will be the case.

We are sure you have heard stories of a manager leaving a company and then many of the agents, if not all from that office, following. The agent's day-to-day or "go-to" person for assistance may be the reason they stay with that firm — or, if that key person leaves, why they would consider leaving as well. On day one of the transaction's announcement, the competitors will be ramping up their efforts to recruit the best sales agents, members of the management team, and even key employees.

We always recommend that the buyer attempt to "lock up" key employees before the closing. This can be a contingent part of the letter of intent (LOI). We have worked with transactions where the seller was required to give a portion of the down payment or earn-out over a period of years through an employment agreement to ensure the continuity of key people. The seller may balk at this approach, but it is also in their best interest (because of the earn-out) that all key staff and agents stay and support the transition.

We have been involved in transactions where the buyer renegotiated the compensation upward of key people and signed employment agreements at closing. It is also common practice in an employment agreement to ask for a non-compete; just know that the amount of compensation that is directed for the non-compete must be noted and fair (which is a very gray area in the courts). A lot of times, non-competes with non-owners may not be enforceable, but they put the person on notice that it may not be easy, and it could harm their reputation or even cost them some money, to join another firm close by.

The same ask for a non-compete would be true if the non-owner was receiving part of the purchase price for their previous or future contributions to the company. Often in the course of a valuation, we will determine that a key person is not being paid market value or their true worth to the organization. If that is the case, we will adjust the profit downward to reflect this. This can be the same for the buyer's offer.

In larger acquisitions, there is often the dilemma of conflicting policies on office managers. One side allows the managers to personally produce, and the other prefers no personal production from their management team.

This too is a negotiation, or at least the creation of a viable plan to address the situation, that should be handled prior to the closing. Many will create a "grandfathering" period for a gradual change.

Please be aware of the importance to the affected individual and the potential risk to the organization when changing the compensation structure. As in recruiting, you must sell the positive benefits to the person. We have seen some firms guarantee a minimum of what they would have made under the previous compensation program for one or two years when changing the pay structure for certain employees.

Acknowledge The Owner's Hard Work

Almost all entrepreneurs feel they have invested their whole lives into their business, and it is usually true (at least to the current point in their lives). They've given up weekends, nights, vacations, and often missed their children's events, all so they could start and grow their business.

Never underestimate this feeling of dedication, commitment, and the love-hate relationship they may have with the company. It is important to be always empathetic and appreciative of all the time and effort devoted to the business. The owner's efforts over the years may not necessarily result in a higher selling price, but they should be acknowledged and complimented.

A good approach is to say, "Sally, no one could ever pay you back for the time and energy you have put into this business, but that effort has allowed you to get to this stage, and your payback is going to come over the next few years as you continue to be a major part of the new company's success. You created a solid foundation to use as a springboard, and to accelerate your opportunity to achieve the life you have worked so hard for."

Again, it is implied that you are the one to help them get there.

Help The Seller Save Face

It is so easy in an acquisition for the buyer to end up playing the role of the expert, the person who can easily see what the seller did wrong, and who then points out those mistakes. The phrases like, "If you had done this instead," or "You should have done that," or "Here's what I would have done" need to be stricken from your vocabulary when you are negotiating a sale.

Trust us: The seller probably knows what they should have done, and they do not want to hear it from you. There is no need to be critical or to second-guess; it is a surefire way to alienate people, and it can also cost you a potential transaction.

You often never know what the hot-buttons or deal-breakers might be. One of us (the older one) was actually asked to leave an office early in my career.

I was learning the ropes of the M&A business from a hot-shot corporate expert. We were involved in an acquisition in a medium-sized market in Florida of a company we really wanted. We were very close to the closing date, and everything was set. We were getting ready to leave the office when my partner started talking about the need to remodel the office — getting a contractor in to get rid of the beige carpet and replace it with gray, changing the wall colors and curtains, and transforming it to the look he and corporate wanted.

We did not realize it, but this was a "saving face" deal-breaker. The seller's spouse had recently lovingly redecorated the entire office, spending a lot of time, money, and effort. He was insulted by the statement. Even with a great offer, ready to close, the seller was not willing to hurt his spouse's feelings. He literally asked us to leave the office, and the transaction never closed.

Later, the seller told me that he felt if we were contemplating these significant changes before we even owned the company, he could not imagine what we would do to it post-closing.

The moral of this story is that you have no way of knowing how much effort and pride is invested in *any* area of the business. We all know what "saving face" means to the external audience (you want to help the seller look good), but we never know what deep-seated deal-breakers are lurking in a seller's mind.

Saving face might not have anything to do with a big title or more money; it could simply mean not being embarrassed. We always recommend that you propose any changes in a collaborative way. A better approach in this circumstance would have been, "What would you think if we tried to get this office to be more in line with the look and feel of our others?" Then explain what that might mean in real terms.

Even if there was huge push-back, there may have been a solution that would have worked — maybe even involving the spouse in the new design. The look of the office was not even a deal-killer for us at corporate! It was very professional and looked great (just not the right colors). But it turned out to be the last straw for the seller.

Ask For Advice

The above "decorating" fiasco could have been worked out quite easily by asking for help.

Solicit the opinions and advice of the seller; both pre- and post-closing, let them know you respect their expertise and appreciate their assistance. It is a best practice to take and implement the best elements from each company.

Size doesn't necessarily indicate quality. There are many smaller companies that may have a better policy, technology, marketing system, or another part of their operation than a large buyer.

You can assess the quality of these systems and policies through due diligence upfront. One example to help you assess communication policies is to ask: "What would you suggest as the most effective way to communicate this change to your agents, staff, and clients?"

Even if you have done this a dozen times, you may learn about an improvement that will help the announcement go better and, in the process, demonstrate that you are not going to "cast aside" the seller. This is one of the top fears for the seller — that they will not be able to have their voice heard post-closing.

These types of questions, followed by assurances like "Maybe we can come up with a plan together," are great closing-type questions, which we used to call the "assumptive close."

Where else do you go for advice? Using a professional firm can lead to smoother and more successful merger and acquisition transactions. Professional firms have seasoned expertise in the following areas:

1. **Identifying potential acquisition targets:** They can use their experience and knowledge of the market and their network of contacts to identify businesses that may be suitable for acquisition.

2. **Assessing the value of the target brokerage:** They can provide a valuation of the target business based on factors such as financial performance, market conditions, and industry trends.
3. **Negotiating the terms of the deal:** They can help negotiate the terms of the deal, including the purchase price, financing arrangements, and any other conditions that may be relevant.
4. **Facilitating due diligence:** They can help coordinate the due diligence process, which involves evaluating the financial and operational condition of the target business.
5. **Managing the closing process:** They can help ensure that all necessary documents are in order and assist with the closing process to ensure a smooth transition of ownership.

Overall, a professional M&A team can provide valuable assistance to buyers and sellers in the process by bringing their expertise and knowledge of the market to bear on the transaction.

Selling The Vision

Though it is a good idea to ask for the seller's advice regarding future decisions and plans, you should also make it known that you are coming into this acquisition with a current business strategy and the ability to execute it, as well as a clear vision for the future of all companies involved.

You will need to convince the seller that if they become part of your growing organization, everyone will benefit: the new combined company will have greater market share, more listings, more visibility, and a more robust platform. There will be plenty of opportunities for the seller and their agents to enjoy personal and financial growth. At the same time, the seller will have more freedom and a chance to focus more on what they enjoy.

This is all a critical part of the process known as "selling the vision." If you cannot get the seller to believe in a future with you, the transaction will probably not happen — or you will not be able to afford it.

Major new real estate franchise players have grown rapidly in recent years because they have been excellent at selling (and delivering on) the vision. Imagine how hard it is to sell a nationwide network concept to the first 50 or even 100 companies. Their approach is to tell them what they are going to do, show them how they are going to do it, share what tools and support will be available, and demonstrate the passion and expertise to make it happen. It sounds like a great road map for a successful acquisition strategy to us. "Passion with a plan," you might call it.

A great example of this is Glenn Sanford at eXp Realty. He reimagined the real estate office as a virtual community, with no bricks and mortar. In this community, agents are avatars who meet through browsers and communicate through Zoom meetings. Early on, it was hard to imagine what Sanford believed would be a revolutionary new construct for real estate brokerages.

Finally, having provided a number of suggested approaches you can use with a seller and questions to ask, it is important to stress that you should not do any of the dialog in a mechanical fashion. The suggested scripts are not merely techniques designed to manipulate the seller and help you get what you want. The intent is to learn the messaging and then adapt to your style so it helps move the process along and avoid the mistakes we have made in the past.

Long-term relationships must be built on sincerity and trust. For instance, if you ask a seller's opinion just because that is something you read to do in this book, that kind of falseness will show through quickly, especially if you never use any of the suggestions the seller offers. And when that happens, the seller will realize you are trying to manipulate them rather than partner with them, which will turn the relationship sour.

Manipulation and negotiating techniques may work in the short run, but they won't for very long. We really need for you to have the seller's interests in your mind at all times. No matter what you call your acquisition, it will be a partnership or joint venture, and you will need both the sellers and buyers behaving their best for at least three years.

A final thought to keep in mind as you are developing rapport: Be patient, and try to avoid discussing any specific numbers as they relate to purchase price or terms.

The seller is likely to push you for a dollar figure; the first thing they want to know in a conversation about selling is, "How much will you pay me?" You should point out it is premature to talk price or terms until you have established what the future relationship will be; once you both agree on present and future needs and goals, then together you can find a way to make the financial part work. But you should also assure them that when the time comes to present a formal offer, it will be fair to both sides, arrived at together, and that it will maximize the benefit for both.

The fact is, before you can come up with an offer, you will have to do a lot more diligence, which is explained in detail in our next chapter under the heading "Information Gathering." In the meantime, do everything you can to keep the conversation and relationship-building moving forward. Remind the seller that, as critical to both as the dollars are, it is equally important to agree on your ability to work together through mutual goals and the vision for the future.

Cultural Compatibility

We are discussing cultural compatibility at the end of the relationship-building section, but before the information-gathering chapter — because this should be investigated at all levels of the organization, from the first meeting, through diligence, to closing. "Culture" encompasses both any expectations for behavior and also the business model. To us, cultural compatibility and the owner's and agent's alignment to yours is a deal-maker or deal-breaker.

How do you determine compatibility? Firms that are similar in model and offering are preferred; they do not need to be totally aligned, but the closer, the better the chance of long-term success.

What does "similar" mean? The areas where large differences are the most difficult to overcome include compensation, support, or business model. It is easier to integrate and retain agents when they feel they are moving to an improved situation, even if it is just a perception you create. It can be a better environment, facility, management, support, tools, training, reputation, or even just straight compensation improvement if that is all you offer.

The acquired agents are typically predisposed to want to stay, but understand that they also do not like a lot of changes. If you are able to minimize the minor changes to a few, and disclose any major changes to none, you are better off.

We have found it very difficult, if not impossible, to modify an agent's compensation program downward — even if you offer more services. It has been done, but it is a very risky proposition, and the seller should be a part of the conversation. Agents leaving will negatively affect you both.

Ideally, you would want to find a smaller firm to acquire, especially for your first transaction. Consider what size firm you and your team can practically absorb and support successfully. Is it 5 agents, 10, or 50-plus with multiple offices? We have worked with smaller companies acquiring much larger ones, but that is not usually the norm, nor is it easy to do.

No matter the size, you must answer the question "Can you integrate this firm into your culture?" An extreme example of it being very difficult would be if you view your firm as a unified team, hold many family gatherings, outings, and sing kum-ba-ya at weekly sales meetings. All of a sudden, you drop a group of acquired agents in your office who have the exact opposite mindset — maybe they are lone wolves who will do a deal at any cost, and you are not able to convert them. You could lose the culture you have created, or more importantly, some of your agents.

On the positive side, the culture or work ethic that the new agents bring in can often be a positive motivator for your existing agents. A few new agents who are excited by your offering can spark excitement throughout the company.

Larry Rideout, Chairman of Gibson Sotheby's International Realty, with his partner Paul McGann have grown their fine firm through multiple acquisitions of all sizes. Larry told us, "Most of our acquisitions have worked out extremely well, adding quality agents and management talent. We get better with each one, but we do know that culture and model similarity are the two most important components of a successful acquisition."

He went on to tell us: "The couple of acquisitions that did not go well, we knew were a stretch; we should have listened to our instincts. One was a dramatically different culture, and the other was a different business model regarding the agents' compensation method. Both had more agents depart than we would have liked."

We have witnessed Larry's experience with many other firms, trying to fit the proverbial "square peg into a round hole." It can be done, but it may not be worth the maximum effort that will be required, nor the risk associated with it.

Long-term retention of the acquired agents (and your existing ones) will determine if your acquisition was worthwhile financially. This is why we believe that cultural compatibility is one of the top priorities for a successful transaction.

Even if you feel you have significantly overpaid for a company, if the agents stay and are productive and positive additions to your team, it will likely be a very successful transaction financially for you.

We have worked with companies that have had the acquired agents stay productive for 10-plus years and are still there. Those owners reaped huge financial and cultural benefits from the acquisition.

Relationship Building:

Considerations To Never Forget

1. Spouse or significant other: Involve early and often
2. Silent partners and investors
3. Employees: Seller usually wants to take care of them
4. Sales and/or office manager(s): The keys to agent acceptance of any transition

5. Acknowledge the seller's hard work and focus on positives
6. Help the seller save face
7. Be humble about everything; don't boast
8. Be careful of suggesting any changes — you do not own the company yet
9. Ask the seller for advice with any areas of potential duplication or conflict
10. Involve key decision-makers

Chapter 5: Information Gathering And Due Diligence

We will now assume the seller has given you the go-ahead to explore a possible future relationship. As the next step in the process, you will begin accumulating information on the prospective candidate and conducting your due diligence.

People often ask us, "How much information do you need before you are in a good position to evaluate a company?" The answer is: As much as you can get. In the information-gathering stage, which starts with the first meeting, you are trying to assemble as complete a picture as possible of the potential company that you want to acquire.

This means that you should not approach this task in a one-dimensional manner — for example, by focusing only on the financial documents. Those documents only tell a part of the story. To really understand the company, you must look further by gathering samples of the company's marketing, training, onboarding, and recruiting materials, and even the policy manuals and customer satisfaction surveys, if possible.

This kind of "holistic" approach to information-gathering is somewhat non-traditional; many acquisition people tend to concentrate only on the financial details. Yes, the numbers are important, but also important is understanding the culture, services offered, agent expectations, and overall business platform. The numbers compiled will tell you how much the company is worth — but also, you are seeking to determine the firms' compatibility.

Start With An NDA

A non-disclosure agreement (NDA) is a legally binding document that prohibits one party from disclosing confidential information. In the context of M&As, NDAs are often used to protect the confidentiality of any sensitive information that is shared during the M&A process, as well as the deal itself.

There are several reasons why NDAs are important in M&A transactions:

1. **Confidentiality:** M&A transactions often involve the sharing of sensitive financial and operational information about the target company. An NDA helps to ensure that this information is not disclosed.

2. **Competitive advantage:** M&A transactions can give the acquiring company a competitive advantage if the deal is successful. An NDA helps to prevent competitors from learning about the transaction and potentially using the information to gain an advantage.

3. **Legal protection:** An NDA can provide legal protection for both the acquiring company and the target company in the event that confidential information is disclosed in violation of the agreement.

4. **Trust:** An NDA helps to establish trust between the parties involved in the M&A transaction and can facilitate the exchange of sensitive information.

SAMPLE NON-DISCLOSURE AGREEMENT

(Please seek your own legal advice before using)

THIS NON-DISCLOSURE AGREEMENT (the "Agreement"), effective _____ ("Effective Date"), is entered into by and between _____ (The Company) a _____ _____ corporation with a principal address at _____ _____ ("The Company"), and the _____(*The Sending Company*), a _____ corporation with a principal address at ___ _____ ("*The Sending Company Name*").

The Company and _____ (*The Sending Company*), specifically agree as follows:

1. <u>General</u>. In connection with the consideration of a possible business transaction (a "Transaction") between The Company and _____ (*The Sending Company*) both parties expect to make available to one another certain nonpublic information concerning their respective business, financial condition, operations, assets, and liabilities. As a condition to such information being furnished to each party and its directors, officers, employees, agents, or advisors (including, without limitation, attorneys, accountants, consultants, bankers, and financial advisors) (collectively, "Representatives"), each party agrees to treat any nonpublic information concerning the other party (whether prepared by the disclosing party, its advisors or otherwise and irrespective of the form of communication) which is furnished hereunder to a party or to its Representatives now or in the future by or on behalf of the disclosing party (herein collectively referred to as the "Evaluation Material") in accordance with the provisions of this Agreement, and to take or abstain from taking certain other actions hereinafter set forth.

2. (2) Evaluation Material. The term "Evaluation Material" also shall be deemed to include all notes, analyses, compilations, studies, interpretations, or other documents prepared by each party or its Representatives which contain, reflect, or are based upon, in whole or in part, the information furnished to such party or its Representatives pursuant hereto which is not available to the general public. The term "Evaluation Material" does not include information which (i) is or becomes generally available to the public other than as a result of a breach of this Agreement by the receiving party or its Representatives, (ii) was within the receiving party's possession prior to its being furnished to the receiving party by or on behalf of the disclosing party, provided that the source of such information was not known by the receiving party to be bound by a confidentiality agreement with or other contractual, legal, or fiduciary obligation of confidentiality to the disclosing party, (iii) is or becomes available to the receiving party on a non-confidential basis from a source other than the disclosing party or any of its

Representatives, provided that such source was not known by the receiving party to be bound by a confidentiality agreement with or other contractual, legal, or fiduciary obligation of confidentiality to the disclosing party or any other party with respect to such information, (iv) is disclosed by the disclosing party to a third party without a duty of confidentiality, (v) is independently developed by the recipient without use of Evaluation Material, (vi) is disclosed under operation of law, or (vii) is disclosed by the recipient or its Representatives with the discloser's prior written approval.

3. Purpose of Disclosure of Evaluation Material. It is understood and agreed to by each party that any exchange of information under this agreement shall be solely for the purpose of evaluating a Transaction between the parties and not to affect, in any way, each party's relative competitive position to each party or to other entities. It is further agreed, that the information to be disclosed to each other shall only be that information which is reasonably necessary to a Transaction, and that information which is not reasonably necessary for such purposes shall not be disclosed or exchanged. In addition, competitively sensitive information, such as information concerning product development or marketing plans, product prices or pricing plans, cost data, customers, or similar information which has been determined to be reasonably necessary to a Transaction, shall be limited only to those senior executives and Representatives who are involved in evaluating or negotiating a Transaction or approving the value of a Transaction.

4. Use of Evaluation Material. Each party hereby agrees that it and its Representatives shall use the other's Evaluation Material solely for the purpose of evaluating a possible Transaction between the parties, and that the disclosing party's Evaluation Material will be kept confidential and each party and its Representatives will not disclose or use for purposes other than the evaluation of a Transaction any of the other's Evaluation Material in any manner whatsoever; provided, however, that (i) the receiving party may make any disclosure of such information to which the disclosing party gives its prior written consent and (ii) any of such information may be disclosed to the receiving party's Representatives who need to know such information for the sole purpose of evaluating a

possible Transaction between the parties, who are provided with a copy of this letter agreement and who are directed by the receiving party to treat such information confidentially.

5. <u>Non-Disclosure</u>. In addition, each party agrees that, without the prior written consent of the other party, its Representatives will not disclose to any other person the fact that any Evaluation Material has been made available hereunder, that discussions or negotiations are taking place concerning a Transaction involving the parties, or any of the terms, conditions, or other facts with respect thereto (including the status thereof) provided, that a party may make such disclosure if in the written opinion of a party's outside counsel, such disclosure is necessary to avoid committing a violation of law. In such event, the disclosing party shall use its best efforts to give advance notice to the other party.

6. <u>Required Disclosure</u>. In the event that a party or its Representatives are requested or required (by oral questions, interrogatories, requests for information or documents in legal proceedings, subpoena, civil investigative demand or other similar process) to disclose any of the other party's Evaluation Material, the party requested or required to make the disclosure shall provide the other party with prompt notice of any such request or requirement so that the other party may seek a protective order or other appropriate remedy and/or waive compliance with the provisions of this letter agreement. If, in the absence of a protective order or other remedy or the receipt of a waiver by such other party, the party requested or required to make the disclosure or any of its Representatives are nonetheless, in the opinion of counsel, legally compelled to disclose the other party's Evaluation Material to any tribunal, the party requested or required to make the disclosure or its Representative may, without liability hereunder, disclose to such tribunal only that portion of the other party's Evaluation Material which such counsel advises is legally required to be disclosed, provided that the party requested or required to make the disclosure exercises its reasonable efforts to preserve the confidentiality of the other party's Evaluation Material, including, without limitation, by cooperating with the other party to obtain an appropriate protective order or other reliable

assurance that confidential treatment will be accorded the other party's Evaluation Material by such tribunal.

7. <u>Termination of Discussions</u>. If either party decides that it does not wish to proceed with a Transaction with the other party, the party so deciding will promptly inform the other party of that decision. In that case, or at any time upon the request of either disclosing party for any reason, each receiving party will promptly deliver to the disclosing party or destroy all written Evaluation Material (and all copies thereof and extracts therefrom) furnished to the receiving party or its Representatives by or on behalf of the disclosing party pursuant hereto. Notwithstanding any language to the contrary, the parties may retain one copy of intellectual or proprietary information for legal or record retention purpose. Each party and its Representatives will continue to be bound by its obligations of confidentiality and other obligations hereunder.

8. <u>No Representation of Accuracy</u>. Each party understands and acknowledges that neither party nor any of its Representatives makes any representation or warranty, express or implied, as to the accuracy or completeness of the Evaluation Material made available by it or to it. Each party agrees that neither party nor any of its Representatives shall have any liability to the other party or to any of its Representatives relating to or resulting from the use of or reliance upon such other party's Evaluation Material or any errors therein or omissions therefrom. Only those representations or warranties which are made in a final definitive agreement regarding the Transaction, when, as and if executed, and subject to such limitations and restrictions as may be specified therein, will have any legal effect.

9. <u>Definitive Agreements</u>. Each party understands and agrees that no contract or agreement providing for any Transaction involving the parties shall be deemed to exist between the parties unless and until a final definitive agreement has been executed and delivered. Each party also agrees that unless and until a final definitive agreement regarding a Transaction between the parties has been executed and delivered, neither party will be under any legal obligation of any kind whatsoever with respect to such a Transaction by virtue of this letter agreement except for the matters specifically agreed to herein.

For purposes of this paragraph, the term "definitive agreement" does not include an executed letter of intent or any other preliminary written agreement. Both parties further acknowledge and agree that each party reserves the right, in its sole discretion, to provide or not provide Evaluation Material to the receiving party under this Agreement, to reject any and all proposals made by the other party or any of its Representatives with regard to a Transaction between the parties, and to terminate discussions and negotiations at any time.

10. <u>Waiver</u>. It is understood and agreed that no failure or delay by either party in exercising any right, power, or privilege hereunder shall operate as a waiver thereof, nor shall any single or partial exercise thereof preclude any other or future exercise thereof or the exercise of any other right, power, or privilege hereunder.

11. <u>Customer Privacy and Non-Solicitation</u>. Each party expressly acknowledges and agrees not to disclose, share, rent, sell, or transfer to any third party any personal or financial information relating to the other party's customers (including without limitation a consumer's first and last name, physical address, ZIP code, email address, phone number, Social Security number, birth date, and any other information that itself identifies or when tied to the above information, may identify a consumer), except as specifically required to satisfy the disclosing party's contractual obligations to the other party, provided that such disclosure would not violate existing law or the privacy policy of either party. Each party also agrees not to contact, solicit, or advertise, telemarket or e-mail to any of the other party's customers.

12. <u>Solicitation of Employees</u>. Each Party agrees that for a period of twelve (12) months immediately following the termination of discussions with the other Party for any reason, whether with or without cause, shall not either directly or indirectly solicit, induce, recruit, or encourage any of the other Party's employees to leave their employment, or take away such employees, or attempt to solicit, induce, recruit, encourage or take away employees of the other Party, either for the Party or for any other person or entity.

13. <u>Miscellaneous</u>. Each party agrees to be responsible for any breach of this agreement by any of its Representatives. No failure or delay

by either party in exercising any right, power, or privileges under this agreement shall operate as a waiver thereof, nor shall any single or partial exercise thereof preclude any other or further exercise of any right, power, or privilege hereunder. In case any provision of this agreement shall be invalid, illegal or unenforceable, the validity, legality, and enforceability of the remaining provisions of the agreement shall not in any way be affected or impaired thereby.

14. <u>Injunctive Relief</u>. It is further understood and agreed that money damages would not be a sufficient remedy for any breach of this letter agreement by either party or any of its Representatives and that the non-breaching party shall be entitled to equitable relief, including injunction and specific performance, as a remedy for any such breach. Such remedies shall not be deemed to be the exclusive remedies for a breach of this letter agreement but shall be in addition to all other remedies available at law or equity. In the event of litigation relating to this letter agreement, if a court of competent jurisdiction determines that either party or any of its Representatives have breached this letter agreement, then the breaching party shall be liable and pay to the non-breaching party the reasonable legal fees incurred in connection with such litigation, including an appeal therefrom.

15. <u>Governing Law</u>. This Agreement shall be governed by and construed in accordance with the laws of the State of (STATE), applicable to agreements made and to be performed within such State.

AGREED AND ACCEPTED

The Company   (*The Sending Company*)

_____   _____

By: _____   By: _____

Title: _____   Title: _____

Date: _____   Date: _____

Seeking Compatibility

Reviewing the various company literature can tell you a lot about compatibility. However, you must back this up with discussions with the owner, other management personnel, and any remaining key stakeholders.

We have all seen wonderful policy manuals that are not followed and even marketing materials that are never used — or the agents never get trained on how to use them. If you feel the company is not up to your standards, this does not mean you write the company off. This may be an opportunity to provide the agents with the tools, direction, and support that they have not received in the past.

On the flip side, there is always the possibility that the seller is the one with better materials, support, and overall offerings. There are two ways this can go: Maybe you will be able to learn from and improve your own offering, or maybe the candidate firm is not making any money because they are offering high commission splits and an incredible amount of services.

This scenario must be treated with a plan to integrate the agents successfully with minimum risk. As we have stated before, it is hard to take away perceived benefits from agents without offering a very good alternative. We have heard of a firm where the agents revolted because the owner changed the coffee service provider.

It is always a good idea during this phase to prepare a comparison of the products and services offered to each company's agents and the corresponding costs and compensation programs. In any case, you do not want to be blindsided by these kinds of operational differences; you should be aware of them going into the acquisition with a plan prepared in advance.

Below is a chart that will provide an idea of areas to compare.

SAMPLE COMPANY COMPARISON

	Your Company	Candidate
1. Commission Schedule		
2. Agent Fees		
3. E&O, Other Insurance		
4. Commission Payment (timing/method)		
5. Brand/Network Offering		
6. Facility- location, parking, workspace		
7. Agent vs. Company provided (i.e. signs, lockboxes, etc.)		
8. Management Support		
9. Marketing Support/Materials		
10. Administrative Support		
11. Marketing Materials		
12. Training		
13. Sales Meetings/Events		
14. Dress Code		
15. Website		
16. Technology offering		
17. Policy Manual		
18. Employee compensation & benefits		
19. Office Manager compensation		
20. Other		

Gathering Data

Remember that during the entire process, the seller will also be evaluating you as a potential partner. It is always a good idea to have a list prepared of the items that you would like to review. There is a balance between asking for too much and not getting enough.

We have found that providing a list makes it easier on both sides. Please also know that the amount of the information you need will be determined, in part, by the size of the company you are acquiring. If it is a three-agent company with a relatively low gross commission income (and probably net income, too), then you can shorten your financial info request substantially.

That said, we would keep the cultural compatibility diligence the same, as three of the wrong agents added to your firm could cause a lot of damage.

The larger the company, the greater the financial risk involved; hence the more disclosure and research is required. It should also be noted that if you are doing a fold-in, there is less need for financial operating information and a larger margin for error. On the other hand, if you are taking over existing office operations, you will need to review every line item to determine which monthly expenses need to be added or can be eliminated.

Your diligence will also give you a sense of the financial cycles and trend lines of the business in recent times. Below is a sample initial information request that can be modified for your own needs. If you are able to get the information requested, you will be well on your way to a thorough assessment.

Seller Initial Information Request

1. Legal Name of Business _____
2. Type of Entity: (Circle) C-Corp S-Corp LLC Partnership Sole Proprietorship
3. Ownership: _____ % Owned _____
   _____ % Owned _____
   _____ % Owned _____
4. Website _____

5. Total Number of Offices_____

6. Total Number of Agents_____

7. For Each Office:

Address, Date opened, # of Full Time Agents, # of Sales Desks, Square Footage, Monthly Rent (fair-market if owned), Owned or Rented, Tenant/Landlord Obligations, Lease Expiration Date

Address	Date Opened	# F/T Agents	# of Sales Desks	Square Footage	Monthly Rent	Owned Y or N	Fair Mkt Rent	Lease Exp. Date

8. Assets: List and provide a description of any wholly owned subsidiaries, joint ventures, and related entities of the company or owner. Include a description of your mortgage and title and escrow operations or relationships.

9. Employees: List all employees, including both part-time and full-time staff. Provide a company organizational chart. Document the following for each employee: Position and responsibilities (for confidentiality purposes, the name is not required), office, hire date, salary or hourly rate, hours per week, annual bonus, other compensation, total compensation.

Position	Name	Office	Hire Date	Salary/ Hourly Rate	Hrs/Week	Bonus	Other Comp.	TOTAL

10. Benefits Plans: Describe type, scope of coverage, participation levels, termination clauses, and costs associated with any plan, including 401(k)s, healthcare, pension, vacation, and so on.

11. Technology: Describe corporate internet and social media strategy and costs ,including website capabilities, portals used for listings, and software utilized for accounting and management programs, agent tools, and support.

12. Agent Splits: What is the average commission charged? (For example, 5%, 4%, 3%)

13. Sales Details: What is the annual agent count, sales volume, sides closed, and average sales price for the last three calendar years?

14. Financial Statements and Balance Sheets: Include this information for a minimum of the past three calendar years for financial statements and the last twelve-month period for balance sheets. (For example, 10/1/22-9/30/23)

    a. On a consolidated basis for the entire company.
    b. At the office level for each office.
    c. For each subsidiary or related entity (i.e., Escrow/Title, Mortgage)

15. Expenses: List and provide a description of all private company expenses ,such as owner(s) compensation, owner sales production and split, owners selling expenses paid by the company, and any perks, such as auto, insurance, country club dues, and so on. Please

include any non-recurring income, such as a large consulting payment, or one-time expenses, such as an office remodel. In doing so, identify the income or expense line item where it was recorded.

16. Agreements: Are you currently under agreement with any national or local franchise, network, or brand (for example, Keller Williams, CLeadingRE)? If so, please provide a copy of the agreement, expiration date, and all fees paid to the affiliation, network, or franchise.

17. Agent Deep Dive: Using a chart similar to the one below, provide a list of sales associates (including any owner(s) who contribute to the production of the brokerage) and their gross commission income and commission earnings for the last twelve months (LTM). Include their previous three years of production, if available. Please indicate the agent's current commission split, plus any special commission arrangements. (This can be documented in a separate report). For confidentiality purposes, numbers can be used instead of agent names.

Agent Name/#	2022 GCI	Agent Net	2023 GCI	Agent Net	2023 GCI	Agent Net

18. Commission And Fee Schedules: Include a copy of the company's current commission and fee schedule, indicating any sales associates who are exceptions to the general commission schedule. Document any initial or ongoing fees charged.

19. Policies: Include a copy of your Policy Manual and sample Independent Contractor Agreement.

20. Financial Policies: Is the commission or fee income recorded when closed or when placed under contract (accrual method)? If using accruals, are there adequate provisions for fall-throughs, and are expenses recorded when paid or received?

21. Agent Expenses: What do agents pay?

22. Transaction Or Other Fees: Are there any transaction or other fees being charged? If yes, describe and indicate how much they are and when they are charged — for example, monthly or per transaction.

23. Debt: Is there any debt outstanding? Debt includes all bank indebtedness, non-compete payments, capital leases, remaining office lease obligations, employment contracts outstanding, loans to and from officers or shareholders, and prior acquisitions.

24. Acquisitions: Have there been any acquisitions in the past five 5 years? If there have, describe any remaining purchase price, obligations, and incentives.

25. Legal Liabilities: Are there any current or pending litigations or violations of any kind?

26. Licenses And Franchises: Are there any licensees, franchisees, or sub-franchisees? If yes, please provide a copy of your agreement, details about the financial relationship, and the expiration date.

27. Contracts And Exclusivity: Are there any contractual relationships and/or exclusivity agreements? If yes, what do they involve, and what is the expiration date?

28. Tax Depreciation: Please attach the current tax depreciation schedule for your furniture and fixtures.

A strategy that may help in building trust is to supply the seller with some of the same information that you are asking them to provide to you. This will not only develop confidence in you as a buyer, but it will also provide them with a roadmap and format for how to collect the information.

Remember that you are in recruiting and sales mode throughout the process. Be aware that these information requests can take a lot of preparation time. Asking for the information piecemeal may be less daunting, but we feel it's not as effective, and it's ultimately more time-consuming.

You might also suggest they utilize the services of a professional M&A advisory team. We have found it is very often helpful when completing a transaction for the sellers to be professionally represented. This allows for their representative to educate and work with them about the true earnings of the company.

VALUATION

It is obvious why you should get a current valuation on a company that you are engaging to acquire. While we address the topic of valuations, we want to stress the importance of getting one annually — even if you are a buyer and never intend to sell.

Annual company valuations are recommended for many reasons, including:

1. Benchmarking your growth and initiatives
2. Accountability for ownership and management
3. Succession planning
4. Accurate personal net worth statements (for all sorts of borrowing)
5. Annual bank loan requirements (most serious business loans would require this)
6. Potential addition of a minority partner or an investor
7. Insurance purposes (for example, key man insurance)
8. Estate planning

For most business-owners, your company is your largest single asset. Real estate company owners define a good year in many different ways. There are a number of metrics and key performance indicators (KPIs) that can track the success of a company, such as:

1. Increase in agents
2. Number of transactions

3. Increase in sales volume
4. Increase in revenue/GCI
5. Listing/pending inventory
6. Money in the bank/savings
7. Net operating income

All of these are potentially positive indicators of success, but unfortunately, taken alone or even together, they do not necessarily mean that the company has become more valuable or even made more money this year than last year.

An annual valuation is a great benchmark or reference point, but without one, how will you determine if the annual business plan was a success? Were the improvements, or even the investments made in the business, beneficial or even accretive?

We believe the two most important components of measuring the success of a firm's year are market share growth (measured by comparing the performance against peers) and the EBITDA (earnings before interest, taxes, depreciation, and amortization) growth. Both are core to a valuation and a healthy sustainable business.

Let's examine what a valuation is, and what it is not. Our definition is: the amount that a reasonable buyer would pay a non-distressed seller at a specific a snapshot in time.

A valuation is an estimate of the true worth of the company (less liabilities owed, such as any debt), plus all excess cash and investments. It is a qualitative analysis designed to give a reality check for the business. As we have stated before, there is both an art and a science to the process, hence it is only a qualified estimate.

Getting To A Value

You have now collected a significant amount of the information and are getting closer to the important question everyone wants to know: What is this company really worth, and how much should I pay?

We'll say it again: Performing a brokerage firm valuation is both an art and a science. There are standard data points that can be compared between like-sized companies, which is the science part. The real "art" is analyzing each income and expense line item. The goal is determining what income and expenses are normal, needed, and relevant to the ongoing operations and the generation of the current income.

We strongly recommend that you use a third party to perform the valuation. A successful M&A deal requires making the seller comfortable with the numbers and, ultimately, the end result. There will be much discussion, seller education, and adjustments needed to determine the adjusted EBITDA number. When the process is transparent, the seller is much more likely to feel comfortable with an agreement.

Ideally, the seller and the third party valuing the firm will reach agreement on the EBITDA number. If the seller feels that they are truly earning $500,000 per year, and the buyer believes it is closer to $200,000, then there is no multiple or terms that can bridge the gap. We always want the negotiating debates to be over the purchase price and terms, not the adjusted EBITDA number. To that end, it is our experience that it is much easier for a third party to reach a consensus, which saves the potential buyer from being the "bad guy" in the education process.

Paul McGann, President of Gibson's Sotheby International Realty, uses an outside expert on every acquisitions. Paul shared with us his thoughts: "In using an outside expert, we are not perceived as the people determining the value or questioning the accuracy of their financials. The expert can explain the process to the seller and arrive at an agreed-to and understood adjusted earnings number. We believe this greatly shortens and improves the process. Our success rate has been much higher when bringing in a qualified professional. "

Whether you handle the diligence internally or turn to an expert in valuations, you *must* get this part right. Oftentimes, brokers will rely on their own expertise or instinct as to whether a particular expense seems appropriate. Even if you consider yourself an expert, the financial statement should be reviewed line-by-line, with explanations requested for items you do not understand or that are unclear.

Income & Expense Statements

Income and expense statements, also sometimes called profit and loss (P&L) statements, are typically the cornerstone to your financial diligence. We like to see at least three years' worth of statements. These documents can provide you with a historical picture; the most current will be the most relevant. Rarely (never) have we ever witnessed a P&L statement that accurately reflects the true earnings of the company. With small, privately held "lifestyle" companies, the goal is to reduce the tax consequences as much as possible. We find that all small company P&Ls we have reviewed either substantially understate the true earnings — though some overstate them. We'll share much more on adjusting for correctness later.

It is important to review the financial statements for the last year (or two) month by month; these will show you the more recent ups and downs, and they just might tell you why the owner is considering selling. Often a company may appear to the industry to be strong, but in reality, the income has been in decline. There may be even unpaid bills that show up as a suspiciously low amount in an expense line item in the recent monthly reports.

The monthly reports can help you spot the current trends or highlight any seasonality issues; to provide clarity, it is often helpful to graph the revenue, expenses, and adjusted net operating income on a monthly basis for the last eighteen months to two years, as the below sample shows. If you want to get really sophisticated, plot a trend line on top for your activity and the overall market during the same time period.

Sample Company
18-Month P&L Analysis

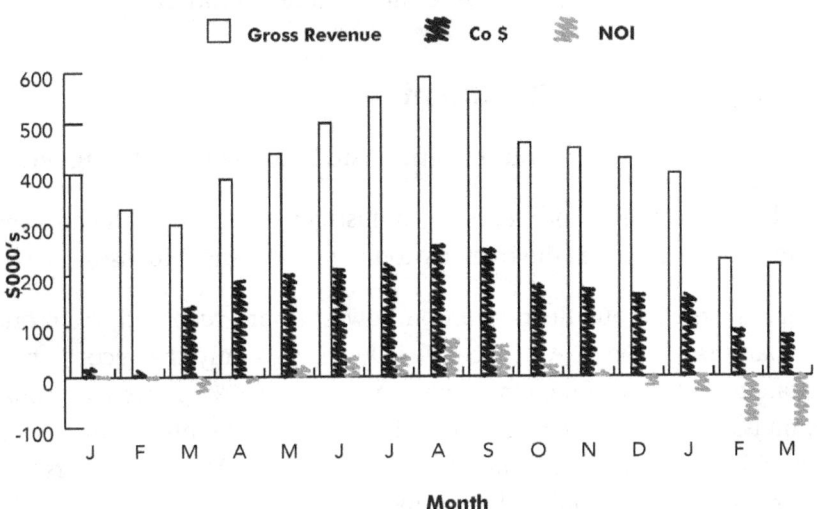

ADJUSTMENTS

Much of what you will see on the financial statement may be the product of wishful thinking, clever accounting, or sometimes unintentional misplaced coding — or even omissions on the part of the bookkeeper or owner. Profit areas may be disguised as expenses, and expenses may be disguised as profit.

For instance, let's say you are looking P&L statements for two companies, and Company A's financials are showing a profit of $200,000 in the past year, while Company B is $400,000. Does that mean that Company B is worth more? Not necessarily; by the time you add back expenses that should have been included, or subtract extraneous expenses — such as a normal commission split for the owner, rather than leaving their entire commission in the company, or a family member's salary, or a boat purchased out of the company — it may turn out that Company A is actually more profitable.

That is the adjustment process in a nutshell: Allowing a true understanding and comparison of the real earnings of a company as if an arm's length "third party" were running the operation.

Major Areas of Adjustment

1. Mysteries of Owner Compensation and Expenses For Management

The biggest variable and necessary adjustment in most small company financial statements is the owner's compensation and expenses.

There is tremendous fluctuation on how both are recorded, from one company to the next. All (usually) is legal; it is only the recording in a statement that differs. One owner may take 100% of their personal commissions out of the company, which reduces the profit number on their P&L statement, while another might leave 100% of their personal commissions in and only take out money as needed, thus inflating the profit number. And there are infinite variations in between.

The owner may take out compensation in a variety of ways, such as a company car, boat, travel, or even paying a family member for a role that they may or may not fill. These may all be prudent business strategies to reduce taxes, but it is part of the reason why financial statements in small companies (and even in some large ones) do not accurately reflect the true profitability of the business.

In particular, you must get a good handle on the owner's compensation method and private company perks. Often the owner is compensated only for their personal production and not for any of their management time. If you are to acquire the company, will you have to pay a branch manager, sales manager, or trainer for roles the current owner might be performing, but for which there is no expense being recorded on the financial statement?

Always be aware of what money will need to be added to provide the same level of service that agents or the sellers currently enjoy as well the perks, such as a boat that will not be needed in the future.

2. Family Member Compensation

As with the owners, there may be a family member who is enjoying similar benefits. Often a family member is on the payroll and receiving excessive compensation for the duties they are performing. The reverse is often true as well, where a family member is performing accounting, operations, or managerial roles without any compensation recorded on the financial statements.

3. Owner(s)/Family Member Personal Sales Expenses

This might be the largest and most frequently adjusted area, dollar-wise.

Many of the companies that you will consider have owners still involved in sales production. We find that many owners leave all their commissions in the company, take out 100% of their commissions, or take money as needed. Each commission method will have consequences on the profit, which will show on the financials, leading to the perception that the seller is generating more profit than is true.

The big challenge is to adjust the past commissions to reflect the commission split program that the seller will be on going forward after the sale. Most owners also group all their personal selling expenses into the company, and those need to be adjusted out if they will not be paid by the company going forward.

As an example, let's say the seller is currently leaving all of their $100,000 commission in the company. Going forward, they will be receiving a 70% split and will pay their own personal sales expenses of $10,000, which are currently paid for by the company. In this example, you would reduce the company profit per the financials by $70,000 for commission to be paid, and then add back $10,000 as profit for personal sales expenses that will be paid by the seller in the future.

4. Owned Offices

We have worked with many sellers who pay less than fair-market rent or no rent at all for their owned offices. Their financials reflect more profit than they should because if they were to sell, they would want to charge fair market rent for the offices thus increasing the actual "run rate" of expenses.

The reverse is also true, where sellers are paying more in rent than fair-market value, or paying for repairs, maintenance, utilities, and other expenses that would not be charged in a normal ongoing rental arrangement. In these circumstances, the financials are showing less profit than they should.

5. One-Time Expenses or Income

Often we will see a financial statement with a very large increase in income or expenses in a one-year period. These must be closely examined to determine if they warrant an adjustment as a one-time event that is either not sustainable or does not affect the future earnings of the company.

An example we have seen of an income adjustment might be an owner who received a one-time payment for the sale of the local MLS that they had an interest in. This was deemed a one-time event that had no bearing on past or future revenue and was deducted from their revenue for the year.

Continuing with that example, the seller might have hired an expensive consultant or attorney to assist with the sale and might have expensed it on their financial statements. This would be adjusted also, and added back as additional profit, because it would be construed to be a one-time expense not germane to the normal brokerage business expenses.

There are many other examples, but the litmus test for a one-time adjustment is: if it had not accrued, would the profitability of the company have been any different that year or in the future?

6. Timing

This includes both seasonality and the LTM financial statement. We have witnessed on more than one occasion a seller who may have a stack of unpaid bills. Timing of revenue accounting and expense-payment recording can alter the look of a small company quite dramatically.

Many statements are prepared on a "cash basis" rather than an accrual basis, so if the owner has not paid $50,000 of current payables, it would actually add $50,000 of profit to the current financial statement that is inflated. They could easily record all the revenue for the month, but not all the expenses.

Even in accrual statements there may be revenue that is recorded that may not come to fruition. This is another very good reason prior to closing a transaction why you should review the current month's activity for any discrepancies in normal expense line items.

If you are able to complete the analysis for the above major adjustment areas, you will be well on your way to performing an accurate valuation.

VERIFICATION

Ultimately, you should verify the financial statements by comparing them to the company's tax return and (if you can) the owner's personal tax returns; you may find that the expenses and income they report to the IRS are dramatically different from the financial statement presented to you. We usually save this verification for a later stage, after the Letter of Intent is accepted; at the sensitive early stages, you do not want to seem as if you do not trust the seller. The old phrase, "trust but verify" is appropriate — and imperative before you close.

What Does The Owner Own?

With regards to facilities, furniture, and office equipment, it is critical to find out exactly what the owner owns and does not own. This is not meant to be funny, but in this day of all sorts of "new age" lease configurations, payment plans, lease options, and annual automatic renewal of agreements, the owner may not know what equipment has been purchased or is on a lease. They may not even know what agreements are auto-renewing.

In our diligence we often find recurring payments for software, equipment, or even office space that is no longer used, and the owner invariably does not realize they are still paying for them.

Tax depreciation schedules are often the best place to investigate the owned assets. It will also tell you how old the furniture or computer equipment is (they should identify the asset, amount purchased, and the date of purchase).

You should review all leases, obligations, and agreements. When it comes to furniture, computers, website hosting, marketing and public relations, and even software, it is surprising how many owners assume they own it or can easily get out of an agreement. In reality, they are dealing with a strong, well-written lease or licensing agreement.

The owner may not be aware of the difference between a lease or a lease with a purchase option, or a straight purchase over time. They may not be aware that they signed a multi-year agreement, or that it automatically renews annually unless 90 days' written notice is given. In addition to the term expirations, it is important to investigate and read the assignment clauses; some may not be assigned without consent, and some may have an assignment fee attached (which can be large), or a mandatory purchase fee if assigned.

If there is a partner or partners involved, it is imperative that you review all internal agreements, including the buy-sell agreement. There may be an impediment to a purchase in those agreements, such as a "first right of refusal" if the company is for sale, or a clause that states all partners are not required to sell, even in a transfer of controlling interest.

If there is any doubt about the agreement or it is a contentious sale among the partners, we would strongly recommend you engage an attorney experienced in working with partnerships and corporate dissolutions.

A broker (who shall remain nameless) told us of their experience with leases. They bought a company for $300,000 cash, with everything included. The owner wanted to sell quickly, and the buyer said it was too good to pass up and did not pursue the full diligence process.

About a month after the close, the bills started to come in. The furniture was all leased (with a large assignment fee), and worst of all, there was an assignment clause in the lease that, without proper notice and approval, voided the agreement. The landlord legally could (and did) make them vacate the office. They acquired some good agents but ended up in a scramble with leased furniture and no location to house those agents.

When a transaction is "too good to be true" ... it usually lives up to the adage. Find and read every lease, membership arrangement, and agreement. If the seller is or was a member of a network or a franchise, review the agreement. Make sure they are out, do not owe any money, and that they have a signed release.

Interfering in agreements, even if you do not know about them, can lead to some serious legal issues. You should not be talking in-depth with a seller who is part of a franchise agreement that has more than one year remaining. It is okay to discuss the possibility of coming together after the conclusion of their agreement, but you do not want to be construed in any way to be inducing or helping them break their agreements. Does "tortuous interference" sound bad? It is — and it will be expensive.

Review every independent contractor agreement the seller has signed with their agents as well as employment agreements with their staff. Are they legal, and are there any ongoing obligations you should be aware of? Will a "change of control" of the company trigger any payments to staff or managers? Will the listing agreements transfer to you as the new owner and broker of record, or will each client need to sign a new agreement? This can be done, but it is better to know before you get a call after closing from the local Board or MLS telling you the listings are all now invalid.

Agent Production

Agent past performance and production is an area that requires close scrutiny.

Getting historical information on all the agents individually is critical. You are hopeful that the production is evenly distributed, with no agent or team producing more than 10% of the overall GCI. You want to see who has been increasing and decreasing their production over the past few years and months. You will want to get start dates with the company, but you'll need to dig a little deeper to find out years in the business.

All of this will give you a sense of the agent retention rate and mix of production. Often you will hear the term "quality of earnings" in discussions of value for a particular company. An ideal breakdown of production in a company is to have 1/3 from high to top performers, 1/3 from average to middle producers, and 1/3 from new or raising star agents. You are looking for a sustainable and stable group of agents who will not be severely impacted if one or two (even if they are top performers) depart for any reason.

Of course, this ideal mix is not always possible, and we have purchased companies where 50% of the revenue comes from a top performer or a team. We would require that the seller assist in some contributing way to "lock-in" for an extended period of time (through an agreement) the key agent(s) by sharing in the purchase price. We would make this a contingent requirement to close the transaction.

If there is one or two agents that are key to the success of the transaction going forward, it is often important to get them on board before the closing. It is understandable that the seller may not want to do this, but if everything else is agreed to, it is in the best interests of both parties.

We were involved recently in assisting a buyer purchase a quality commercial brokerage and property management company. There were two young, hard-charging agents who comprised about 40% of their production. They were type of agents you wanted to build a company around. We felt that the seller should offer these two some monetary compensation for agreeing to stay on through the earn-out, which was three years. The seller disagreed and did not even want to bring them into any conversations.

We wanted to include them because the buyer was going to provide a prominent local and national brand, a great reputation, a marketing department, and much more support than the seller had been providing. This was also a big reason why the seller was confident the two agents would stay and not be a problem — because the two agents had been asking for all of these items (for quite a while, we later learned.) This lack of locking up the key agents was a huge sticking point in the negotiations for us and the buyer.

The company was to be instantly accretive to the buyer, and they really wanted to do the transaction. Finally, we were able to create an earn-out that satisfied the buyer in case the two agents left at any time. You have probably already guessed the end to this story, but about a week before the closing, the two top agents departed to another firm (not as good) that was offering the services they had been asking for ... but unbeknownst to them, they were only two weeks away from getting everything they wanted in their current environment.

Even after they left, all the seller would tell them (and the rest of his existing agents) was to "please stick around" and that "there are some big improvements on the horizon." Unfortunately, the seller had been saying this for years without any change.

Weeks later, we talked to the departed agents, trying to get them back, and they said if only they had known, things would be different, and they would have stayed — but they accepted a signing bonus from the new company and were now obligated. As a result, the transaction was re-traded at a far lower purchase price, and it did ultimately close — with much less revenue.

The moral of the story is that when a significant component of the value of a firm is really in the control of a non-owner, they need to be treated with respect, communication, and compensation by both the seller and the buyer.

Listing Inventory

If you ask a broker how many listings they have, they may say "about 200," but in actuality they may have 100 or even 300. Again, it's not that they are misleading you; they might not know what their current listing count or mix of inventory is. They usually know the pending sales, or the closings for the week, but often are not as up-to-date on active listings.

Analyzing the listing inventory is important. You want to review the listing inventory over the last two years on an agent-by-agent basis. You want to assess the current state of saleable inventory by price point, property type, days on the market, historic list-to-sale ratio, historic percent of listings that sell, and what agents control which listings.

Are the list prices higher or lower than the market average? Are the ratios in line with industry and your own standards? You should consider not just the quantity of the listing inventory but also the quality and salability of those listings by looking at average days on market compared to other firms.

Pay close attention to the expiration dates, which can tip you off to upcoming agent problems. We are sure you are familiar with the pattern seen when a strong producer gradually or suddenly is running out of their usual inventory. It may indicate a market shift, but it usually is the precursor to a different kind of shift — a shift to another company for the agent. It is at least worth investigating before it happens.

Pending sales will be critical to your cash flow the first few months. Analyze them closely, looking at historical fall-out rates, closing dates scheduled, agents involved, and the expected GCI and company dollars from each. Compare them to the pending sales in prior years and months, looking for any positive or negative trends that could highlight issues within the agent population or possibly just reflect current market conditions. Comparing the seller's current statistics to your firm's pending activity will be both helpful and insightful.

Going By The Book

Well-written policy manuals can tell you a lot about a company, such as:

- Commission Programs
- Independent Contractor Agreements
- Agent Fees and Offering
- Agent Expectations
- Referral Policy

- Marketing/Internet Offering And Guidelines
- Services And Tools Provided

Buyer beware: The policy manual may not be totally in line with reality at the company.

For example, the compensation program may say one thing in the manual, but you should always look for exceptions. While investigating independent contractor agreements, you may find that one agent was given a monthly marketing allowance, another agent was given a higher split, while another had all their owned properties carved out at no commission to the company.

The major problems with policy manuals are tracking down all the exceptions and determining how well the policies are followed or enforced. This will take some digging on your part with the seller or the seller's management team, but is worth it.

You do not want to assume everyone was hired at a certain split only to find out that half of the firm has "special" deals that may or may not be documented in writing. It behooves you to have a discussion about *every* individual agent before closing. You want to understand as much as you can about each one — their history, potential, personality, and strengths, but also if there are any promises or special exceptions that have been made.

Take a close look at commission net sheets to see exactly how the commission is being calculated. Many brokerages have different policies on how expenses are charged to transactions before or after the commission calculation.

Who Does What (Or: Who Really Runs This Company)?

In small, privately held companies, job titles do not necessarily tell you what people really do. Oftentimes, a person's responsibilities at a company go well beyond their title.

Is the administrative person actually acting as the sales manager or running the office? Is there a family member doing the bookkeeping or running the website? And how about the owner's duties — do they encompass everything from plunging clogged toilets to training agents in the field, or is it just personal sales?

We have been involved in many transactions where the roles and duties of a person have been severely under-stated. We were told that the person was "just an admin and easily replaceable" only to find out they were the key piece in keeping the office running and together.

We have also been provided an inflated view of what a person is doing for the firm, when in reality, they were not a significant benefit, and even sometimes a detriment to the firm.

It is important to create your own assessment of what each person is currently doing, and more importantly, what they are capable of doing. We have witnessed employees who have blossomed and thrived under new leadership, and taken on far more expansive roles as their talent was being under-appreciated or under-utilized. Conversely, we have witnessed people who we felt were key contributors not transition well to a new management style of a change in ownership.

We believe it will take at least 60 to 90 days to determine what you have acquired in terms of staff talent. We recommend keeping as many people as possible from the acquired firm until you are confident about who the key contributors are and who you want on your team going forward.

'NEVER FORGET' LIST

Finally, we have come to another checklist, which we call "Considerations to Never Forget." This should be referred to as you are gathering information and performing your due diligence, because it is easy to overlook these:

1. **Policy Manual Vs. Reality:** As mentioned earlier, the two can be worlds apart. It is important to review the manual, but do not take it as the truth.

2. **Leased Vs. Owned Equipment and Agreements:** Do not assume; investigate and read every agreement.

3. **Assignment Clauses:** If the office space, furniture, equipment, or software is leased, always review the assignment clause, preferably getting a release or approval before the closing.

4. **Reallocate Strange Expenses:** Determine through a line-by-line review of the financial statements what expenses are appropriate for the operation and what expenses are not needed going forward.

5. **Be Careful Of Owner's Compensation:** Investigate how commissions are treated currently and solidify the plan going forward. What commission schedule will the owner be given? Is the office owned, and if so, is it at fair-market value? What perks or business expenses will continue for the owner or their family members?

6. **Occupancy Costs:** What will the rent be going forward and the tenants' financial responsibilities?

7. **Analyze Listing Inventory:** Review closely all expiration dates, the inventory mix, and salability by agent. Compare their historical performance and your market knowledge.

8. **Evaluate Pendings:** Identify fall-through rates, company dollar amounts expected, and when — by agent. Compare their historical performance and your market knowledge. Create a cash flow budget for the first 90 days.

9. **Prepare A "Combined Company" Pro Forma:** By a pro forma we are simply talking about using your experience to make an educated guess (projection) of what you believe will happen

with revenues and expenses for the next one to three years. We always recommend creating three projections: Worst Case, Most Likely, and Best Case. It is always a good idea to "stress test" your assumptions by planning for how you would modify expenses if the revenue targets were different than what you expected (which is most likely.) Be sure to include the payments to the seller and the conversion expenses.

A final thought: At this stage, you should take your time and make sure you gather all the information required to make a good decision. When you are in acquisition mode, or "making a deal" mode, it is often tempting to want to push the decision quickly. But it is best to not get rushed at this stage; you will want to do thorough research and gather as much information as you need around both the financial and cultural fit.

If the cultural compatibility feels right at this point, you are ready to proceed to the next critical stage — determining what the company is worth to you.

Chapter 6. Valuation And The Offer

The Pro Forma

The business definition of a pro forma is: "A financial statement that leverages hypothetical data or assumptions about future values to project performance over a time period that hasn't yet occurred."

Our pro forma definition (in English) is: Calculate your best guess of what your financials (profit and loss) will look like next year and in the future if you acquire the target company. You should add all of the projected transition costs into your transition budget, plus any expected seller payments based on performance. Cost savings or synergies should be planned for, itemized, and accounted for in future years. The pro forma is a critical step, especially if increased profitability is the reason for the acquisition.

We recommend that you estimate the first year on a monthly basis to determine your cash flow needs. The first 12 months will probably be your most expensive (in terms of cash outflow) period. There may be severance paid out, moving expenses incurred, additional advertising and promotion, and the normal transition expenses, such as the kick-off party, signs, and website modifications, to name a handful.

Of course, there will be additional revenue and cost savings to budget for, as well. The pro forma can be completed either before or after the valuation. It is ideal for you to use this exercise to assist with both formulating the offer and then detailing the effect the purchase price payments will have on your cash flow.

Below is a very simplified sample pro forma for three years to help understand the concept. We would recommend using your current financial statement as the model, utilizing the line items to forecast where the additional revenue, cost savings, and expenses will be recorded on the statement.

As in the example, rarely are all the synergies realized in the first 12 months. It is our experience that you should plan for the cuts, but keep people in place and do not make any non-obvious cuts until the dust has settled and you have evaluated the needs of the combined entity.

In the example, we assumed the purchase price would be $400,000 for Seller Realty, with 25% down at closing. The earn-out payments are esteemed to be $100,000 for each of the next three years. We added transition costs and synergies achieved from a reduction in the seller's headcount. As you can see, by the end of year three, Seller has been paid, and Buyer's company valuation and bottom line have significantly improved. There are no further payments after year three.

This positive financial scenario is achieved in most acquisitions where the buyer is able to retain the vast majority of the agent production.

Pre-Acquisition Pro forma	Seller Realty	Buyer Realty	Est YR1 Combined	Est YR2 Combined	Est YR3 Combined
Revenue:	2,000,000	7,000,000	9,000,000	9,450,000	9,922,500
Cost of Goods Sold:	1,200,000	4,800,000	6,000,000	6,300,000	6,615,000
Gross profit:	800,000	2,200,000	3,000,000	3,150,000	3,307,500
Operating Expenses:	790,000	1,900,000	2,690,000	2,824,500	2,674,500
Operating Income:	10,000	300,000	310,000	325,500	633,000
Adjustments	90,000	50,000	140,000	147,000	154,350
Synergies			75,000	150,000	Ongoing in Exp.
Transition Costs			(50,000)	-	
Adjusted EBITDA	100,000	350,000	475,000	622,500	787,350
Less Seller Payments			200,000	100,000	100,000
Net Cash Flow			275,000	522,500	687,350

Potential Fit

If acquiring a real estate company happened to be a mathematical template, with the pro forma always being right, then this would be the stage at which we would present a foolproof formula for determining the value of the seller's company.

You would then apply the same formula to each and every acquisition in the future. It would all be so simple!

Although we do use formulas on every company valuation, we also need to inject some caution about using them exclusively, because the acquisition process isn't nearly as formulaic (or easy) as running some numbers. Certainly, science and formulas are part of it, and in this chapter, you will be introduced to several formulas that are designed to help you sort through the uncertainties of a company valuation. But those formulas, in and of themselves, will not provide the key to a successful acquisition.

While they will help you place a theoretical dollar value on a company, it is important to remember that valuation formulas are generic. Although they can be invaluable in helping you assess your opportunity, they apply the same equations to every situation, when in fact, every buyer and seller are unique.

Here is an example of uniqueness: Buyer A is willing to pay $500,000 for Zebra Realty and Buyer B $750,000, having seen and arrived at the same earnings for Zebra Realty. The difference may be that Buyer B will immediately be able to make significant expense reductions or synergies moving the agents into an existing office that Buyer A will not enjoy. In fact, Buyer B may derive more profitability even if they pay significantly more for the company. In theory and by formula Zebra Realty is worth $500,000, but the special circumstances may allow Buyer B to pay more — not that they necessarily will, but they could.

For this reason, formulas do not always address well the specific needs of a particular buyer and a particular seller. They do not account for the "hidden variables," which we will discuss shortly, that can influence any deal.

Looking past the financial aspects, they do not address the possibility of a "culture clash" after the sale, which can render the formulas and projections completely moot. Often, they do not deal with the critical issue of risk, such as a different business model, agent defections, or the agents' perception of the offering — risk that is inherent in any acquisition.

In this chapter, while presenting a variety of formulas to assist you in the process, we will also deal with these other issues that are central to determining how much you can pay and how you pay it. We will show you the best methods to adjust for risk and the variables unique to the business.

But know that in the end, the process is about the humans involved in the transaction, and their loyalty, retention, and future productivity.

Pricing

If there is one key point that should be stressed at the outset of any discussion about value, it is this: There is no "exact price" for any given company.

If someone tells you your company is worth $2,342,578.85, then there is a good chance they have used a common formula … but they are also probably guessing.

The reason there can be little true consensus down to the dollar (or cents) of what any company is worth has to do with the nature of the real estate business, which is localized, specialized, and dependent on all sorts of intangibles. Hence the example above, where Zebra Realty was worth more to one buyer than another.

We have seen companies pay much more for a business then the valuation would warrant, but years later it was a huge financial success. Conversely, we have worked with companies that have paid far less than the valuation would warrant for a company, and because of agent and staff defections, it was a financial disaster.

Once again, we remind you to view the formulas that will be presented as guidelines, not gospel; they will help you set the parameters of value, at which point your belief in the cultural compatibility of the two firms and your ability to retain the agents will weigh heavily on the negotiations and the ultimate decision.

Factoring "Breakage"

As we have discussed quite a bit (for a reason), the ultimate success of an acquisition depends greatly on what occurs after you purchase a company.

There is a term in the acquisition vernacular called "breakage." Just know that "breakage" is bad. This is when agents depart after closing.

In previous corporations for which we have acquired firms, we would always prepare a financial pro forma or model with a breakage factor. It was felt in very large acquisitions that if we were able to keep 95% or more of the GCI pre-closing, we would be pleased. Anything over 5% of the GCI departed, and it was a concern — and over 10% was a real problem.

We recommend that you hope for the best and plan for the worst. You should always run your projections with your "most likely" case having a base of a 5% reduction. With a well-executed communication and integration plan, we are hopeful that you will not lose anyone. The agents are predisposed to want to stay.

Create a risk assessment and be aware that if you are implementing radical changes — such as closing an office, changing commission plans, or even offering a perceived "lesser" brand of coffee — you may experience some defections.

Just ask Len Davis (whose name has been changed here), a California-based broker who saw one of his acquisitions turn into a small-scale "civil war" right inside his own office.

"We acquired a company that was used to a different level of tools, a much looser management style, and then moved them into our office," says Davis. "The new agents skipped meetings, did not try to blend in, complained about everything. Meanwhile, we were trying to create a family culture and upscale image for our company."

The result was resentment between the agents, both old and new, leading to significant defections from each side. Says Davis: "I thought I could change them, and I did not see the warning signs. If I go looking for another company in the future, I am going to look much more closely at the culture and make sure they are compatible."

What causes cultures to be mismatched? As we all know, every real estate company — and even different offices within that company — have a distinct personality, which are often a reflection of the local leadership and the owner. You can tell a lot about culture by the way the broker and agents operate.

Your own agents have probably done transactions with them. Often, the level of professionalism shown by agents when dealing with representatives of a competing company is a good indication of how they work with fellow agents within their own company.

Will The Two Groups Work Together?

At some point, after you have gotten a feel for the seller's culture, you must ask yourself the following questions: "Can I make this integration successful? And what effect will it have on my agents, my staff, and on me?"

This should be considered from both an operational and financial standpoint: Can the administrative support handle the additional people? Will your facilities accommodate the increased use?

Even in the best of circumstances, it is a lot of work to integrate and assimilate a large group of agents. But keep this in mind, too: If you do not do an acquisition, your only means of achieving comparable growth is a mass recruiting effort. How much time and resources would *that* take, by comparison?

Even with the significant effort, time, and resources required to achieve a successful acquisition, we believe it is the fastest and most effective way to grow a company.

The Formulas: How Much Can You Pay?

After determining that a company will be a good fit, it is time to begin evaluating the target based on the numerical information you have gathered; at this point, you may begin to apply one or more of these formulas to assist with the valuation.

We are presenting formulas that are talked about and claim to be used in the industry. We have only ever successfully used the Market-Based Valuation formula on more than 1,000 valuations and transactions for existing companies. (We will confess that on two occasions we used the Discounted Future Earnings Approach for start-up companies that had no historical information.)

Bottom line, we believe that using the adjusted EBITDA based on historical results is the only formula we would endorse and recommend. We have also been told that some firms have used a percentage of revenue or GCI to determine value. We would strongly discourage this, as there is no accommodation for profitability.

However, in case you hear of these other approaches, we wanted you to know what they involve (and why it's best not to use them).

1. **Net Asset Value:** Focusing exclusively on the value of the asset base of the firm found on the balance sheet. Typically, this model will produce the lowest valuation.
2. **Discounted Future Earnings:** Focusing exclusively on the estimated earnings potential of the firm. In most, but not all cases, this approach will produce the highest valuation. Could be used in new firm valuations, although projections are often risky.
3. **Assets and Earnings:** Combining the two previous models in an attempt to find some mid-range valuation point.
4. **Per-Listing Valuation:** This approach is often used in small acquisitions where the agents are folded in to the acquiring firm. It takes into consideration the percent of historical income from listings and sales.
5. **Market-Based Valuation:** This formula is the industry standard and uses industry comparables to derive valuation for like-sized companies based on a multiple of earnings times the adjusted EBITDA, which often includes the weighting of previous years.

Net Asset Value

The net asset approach bases the valuation upon the size of the asset base that has been created as a result of past operations. In the simplest terms, it represents the liquidation value of the firm. In most instances, this approach will produce the lowest estimate of the firm's value, particularly for the firm that continually operates at a profit.

The balance sheet provides a basis for determining the net asset value of the firm. This valuation model simply accepts the fact that at time of liquidation, assets may be worth less than the value shown on the books. However, in some instances, assets may actually be worth more.

The valuation involves multiplying each asset category by the adjustment factor. For example, cash is worth 100% of its stated value, but accounts receivable are valued at between 85% and 95% of their book value, depending on historic collection issues. Adjustments and judgements are made based on experience, along with feedback from the company's controller.

After the adjusted value of the assets are all added together, all liabilities are subtracted to determine the Net Asset Value. Again, this approach really does not take into consideration the profitability of a firm.

In the analysis, a couple of points are essential:

1. Inventory is shown on a first in, first out (FIFO) basis
2. Loans from shareholders are excluded from liabilities and are transferred to equity.

Discounted Future Earnings

This model, sometimes called Discounted Cash Flow (DCF), suggests that the value of the business is better measured by looking at the current and future earnings stream of the business using the concepts of the time value of money.

An example is as follows: You would estimate that the company will earn $100,000 in year five, and then depending on the discount factor, determine what that means in today's dollars.

There are two inherent challenges in this process:

1. Determining actual earnings and projecting them in the future.

2. Determining the current value of the future earnings stream to a buyer today, or the discount factor.

In a real estate brokerage valuation, the cash flow used in the projections would be the adjusted EBITDA. You also need to estimate the purchase price (outflow), annual discounted EBITDA, and the terminal value of the firm in a future potential sales year.

Assets And Earnings

This method is commonly used in valuation methodologies across multiple industries (not real estate). In very simple terms, it involves a combination of the two previous models. That is, it assumes the buyer is purchasing both the inherent value of the assets plus a future earnings stream.

The asset component of the calculation is identical to that used in the net asset value method. That is, the buyer is paying for the net value of the company's assets.

The earnings component is equally direct and comes from the second approach, Discounted Future Earnings. It is simply the discounted value of the anticipated future earnings stream.

This approach is clearly designed to be a compromise. This methodology is frequently used in businesses in industries (non-real-estate) that have high volatility, along with widget-based businesses.

Per Listing

In theory, based on comparable acquisitions in the market, you can determine how much is being paid per listing, and that can serve as a guideline. This works much better in a stable market environment.

Companies have paid anywhere from a low of 20% of the Company Dollar/Gross Profit for listings as they close, up to 100%+. Below is an example of how to calculate the value of the listing inventory. This is also a good method for forecasting a firm's future cash flow based on its current inventory.

CURRENT LISTING INVENTORY VALUATION

Listing Inventory Dollar Volume	$9,100,000
Sales Rate (D)	× .80
=	$7,280,000
Times % of Asking Price (E)	× .93
=	$6,770,400
Times Net Office Commission % (C)	× .013
=	$88,015
Times Turnover Rate (A)	× 3
Divide by 12 Months	/12
Projected Monthly Income From Listings =	$22,003
Divide by % of Income For Listings (B)	/.66
Projected Total Monthly Income =	$33,339
Less Monthly Expense =	$(24,400)
Projected Monthly Profit (Loss) =	**$8,939**
Time in Month Before Income is Received	
(90) Days on Market + (30) Processing Time =	4 Months
30	

A. **Turnover Rate**

The Turnover Rate forecasts the number of times in one year you should receive the projected value of your inventory. It is calculated by dividing 365 (the days in a year) by the average days the inventory is on the market before it is placed under contract.

This measurement reflects the quality of the inventory relative to competitor's properties that are attempting to be marketed, and the speed with which action is taken to make competitive adjustments.

B. **Percent of Income From Listings**

This performance indicator shows how adequately the inventory meets the buying client's needs and how willingly the firm's agents seek cooperation when they do not have what the client wants. It is calculated by dividing your Company Dollar earned on the sale of your listings by your Total Company Dollar.

This measurement is also used to project your Total Commissions.

C. **Net Office Commission**

This indicator expresses the Company Dollar as a percentage of the Sales Price. It is calculated by dividing the Company Dollar (i.e. Gross Commissions, less amounts paid to the agents and other brokers) by the Sales Volume.

It reflects the relationship between Gross Commission, agent splits, and the amount of transactions where the listing and selling agents are both with one company.

D. **Sales Rate**

Sales Rate can be calculated using listing units of their dollar volume. It is determined by dividing the listings sold (closed) by the total listings removed from inventory (including any closed, expired, canceled, or withdrawn by the owner) during a given time period. This reflects the quality of the inventory relative to the competitor's properties that are being marketed.

E. **Percent of Asking Price Received**

This performance indicator may be calculated by dividing the sales price of a listing by its most recent asking price prior to the acceptance offer by the seller. It reflects the quality of the initial pricing, the frequency of competitive adjustments, and the market balance in general.

Market-Based Business Valuation

This is the primary method of valuing real estate brokerage businesses, and it has become an industry standard. The market-based business valuation relies upon the comparison of the subject business to similar residential real estate businesses that have actually sold.

There are several sources of market data commonly used:

- Publicly traded residential brokerage company sales.
- Private residential brokerage company sales.
- Previous sales of the subject business.

We typically use the private residential brokerage company sales data with firms we have direct knowledge of. The companies selected for comparison are closely held firms that resemble the subject business in terms of their financial and operational characteristics.

In established businesses, we normally utilize the Market-Based method, also sometimes called the Comparative Transaction Method, to estimate the value of the subject business. Under this method, we determine the often-mysterious, "pulled from thin air" valuation multiples that relate measures of business financial performance to its potential selling price.

The market multiple we use is similar to the inverse of the capitalization rate. In essence, it is a calculation of how many months or years the buyer wants to get their money invested returned. In evaluating a commercial property, the capitalization rate is calculated by dividing a property's net operating income by its asset value (or purchase price). The cap rate is an assessment of the yield of a property over one year going forward. For example, a property worth $14 million generating $600,000 of NOI would have a cap rate of 4.3%.

In a real estate brokerage firm acquisition, which is a much riskier investment (usually) than a commercial property, we could assume the firm is generating the same $600,000 of adjusted EBITDA. We could continue the example, using the market multiple of 4.3, which would yield a firm value of $2,580,000. Under similar rough comparisons, the commercial property would sell for a 4.3% annual return, where the brokerage firm would sell for a projected 23% return.

Another way to look at the market multiple number is that the buyer wants to get all of their money invested back in 4.3 years. Below are the formula examples.

$$\text{Capitalization Rate} = \frac{\text{Net Operating Income (EBITDA)}}{\text{Purchase Price}}$$

$$\text{Market Multiple} = \frac{\text{Purchase Price}}{\text{EBITDA}}$$

Not to complicate matters, but there is also an external and internal multiple.

The external multiple is the number used to calculate the purchase price based on the acquired company's historical financials. The external number is usually shared with the seller for the sake of transparency and to show how the buyer arrived at the purchase price.

The internal multiple number takes into consideration the potential synergies available to the buyer. Typically, the adjustments and add-backs to profit are the domain of the seller, and any synergies are to the benefit of the buyer outside of the valuation of the potential acquisition.

An example of a seller benefit might be eliminating part or all of a redundant marketing or technology position, absorbing the accounting for the acquired firm into the existing infrastructure, or even the closing of an office. The internal multiple target might be a three, further reducing your risk and leading to an even more profitable acquisition.

As a buyer, this might be a good time to reflect on the understanding that in the above example(without synergies) it will be 4.3 years before you receive the full purchase price back — if the production levels remain flat. In the capitalization rate example, it is often called "fully capitalized." When a buyer tells you that you are not paying enough, you can remind them that per the offer, there is no expectation of any profit distributed to the buyer for at least 4.3 years.

On the positive side, as a buyer, you are hoping the acquired firm will create more revenue than they have historically under your guidance and offering. Ideally, you will also be able to reduce some expenses, absorbing some of the activities of the firm into your existing infrastructure.

The goal is to generate some profit to you for the payout length, and at the end, have an asset worth more than the $2,800,000 you paid for it while reaping the benefit of the entire EBITDA distribution after 4.3 years. We know of no better way to quickly grow a company and build personal wealth at the same time.

A successful and fair-to-both-sides acquisition is directly related to correctly arriving at the adjusted EBITDA and applying the appropriate market multiple. Although a market multiple may look simple, if done correctly, it is a complex assessment of factors, including the firm's historical data, current market conditions, similar recent sales, risk tolerance, and most importantly, buyer return expectations.

For our valuations we use a proprietary algorithm that is a sophisticated mix of researched information. The factors we use to determine the firm's multiple and ultimately its value include:

1. Geographic market
2. Facilities and locations
3. Market share
4. Recent trend lines
5. Average sales price
6. Reputation and quality of target's brand name
7. Historical numbers

8. Quality of earnings and spread of agent production: Not over 10% in any one agent or team
9. Productivity per agent
10. Sustainability
11. Quality of management team
12. Franchise or network affiliation
13. Size: GCI and sales volume
14. Recent market comparable sales
15. Company dollar retention
16. Profit margin
17. EBITDA

There are dozens, sometimes hundreds, of potential decisions that go into the adjusted EBITDA and multiple number creation. However, once the multiple is established, the value of a company is calculated through what is then a simple formula, multiplying the market multiple times the adjusted EBITDA.

Because of the simplistic nature of the formula below, many sellers and sometimes even other consultants do pick a multiple number from "thin air" or use a baseline number that they apply to all companies. Then they compound the error by using whatever the financial statement says the EBITDA is without adjustments.

We have often told audiences at our seminars that you can give a seller almost any multiple they want as long as you control what they are multiplying the number times (EBITDA). The reverse is also true: If the seller is stuck on their EBITDA number without adjustments, then it could be used against you even if you have control of the multiple.

Of course, both scenarios may be far-fetched, but we want to make the point that in a simple formula such as this one, it is amplified and extremely apparent that "garbage in = garbage out."

Market Multiple X Adjusted EBITDA = Brokerage Firm Value

Franchise Or Network Affiliation

We often are asked whether a franchise agreement or network affiliation will help or hurt the value of a firm. The short answer is "yes." It all depends on the circumstances.

If the company has a number of years remaining on their agreement and does not have any "easy-out" or termination clause, then it will limit the number of potential buyers. The only firms that may be interested are companies with the same brand affiliation. It definitely shrinks the buyer pool; however, we have been involved in transactions where a firm was purchased and kept operating with a brand that was different from the purchaser's brand affiliation.

The reverse can also be true. As of this writing, quality firms with strong brands, such as Sotheby's International Realty, are sought out by potential buyers and are receiving a premium in value. Other brands or network firms with desirable territories that may even be protected are also in demand by the similarly affiliated firms or even non-branded companies.

Price vs. Terms

While the valuation formula can provide a target value range to work with, the most critical aspect of the transaction is the terms that you agree upon with the seller, which will dictate how and when the price is paid.

If for example, you determine that the company is worth $1,000,000, you might pay $250,000 down, with the remaining $750,000 on an earn-out over a certain number of years based on the performance of the acquired agents.

Terms and price are interrelated; to get the better of one, you must give up some of the other. Whether you pay a premium price or a minimum price for a company will often depend upon the terms of the deal.

While there is a natural tendency to want to pay the lowest price, getting the right terms may be more important than getting the lowest price. Conceivably, a buyer could acquire a company at a perceived "bargain" price by agreeing to pay the full balance upfront at closing, with no terms. But with a real estate company, that is extremely risky on multiple levels; the agents may or may not come to work for you the next day. No matter how little you paid for the company, it could still be too much.

As a rule, the larger the company, the less risk of meaningful impact from a few defections. It goes to reason that if there are only 10 agents, and 3 of them leave, it could have a significant impact. If there are 100 agents, and 3 leave, it should have minimal impact on the overall gross revenue — unless they are all top producers.

Shared Risk, Maximum Benefit

Because such risks are inherent to real estate acquisitions, it is important for buyers to protect themselves via the process of risk-sharing. At the same time, risk-sharing allows the seller to maximize the value of the company and achieve the highest purchase price.

Typically, the more favorable the terms (earn-out), the more potential purchase price for the seller. By basing the earn-out on the performance of the agents acquired, or the total firm, the risk to the seller is mitigated as the payments will rise and fall based on actual contributions by the acquired agents.

While using the shared risk strategy may increase the price that is ultimately paid for the company, it is the only way we recommend that you purchase a company. If the acquired agents perform based on their historical activity, or if they perform better, then you should be willing to pay a premium as the transaction has been very beneficial for both sides. If the agents or firm under-performs, you are protected as a buyer somewhat with your monetary payments being reduced based on actual production delivered.

Ideally as a buyer, you want to pay for the production only of the agents you acquire. You are paying for the historic performance of each individual agent. Again, you may pay more or less for each agent and the collective of agents, which is all dependent on their actual production during the earn-out.

This individual agent accounting is easier to negotiate and account for with smaller acquisitions. Most "fold-ins" are based on this method; the earn-out is only paid on the agents that are acquired and on the roster at closing. It is almost impossible to base the payout on a total firm methodology when the agents are integrated into the buyer's office.

When existing offices are taken over and kept, it is still a "best practice" to pay only on the specific agents acquired — but this is often negotiable, as sellers want to get credit for *any* agents recruited to that office during the payout period. The logic is that the seller gets credit for the momentum of the office, and in normal circumstances, there would be recruits.

The potential downside for the buyer is that you may be a better recruiter and grow the office much faster than the seller could. The positive is you will have purchased a very healthy and growing office, even if you pay a little more for it.

Terms are risk-adjusted and reflected in the purchase price.

Purchase Price vs. Risk

Sample Purchase Price Range = $300,000 - $500,000

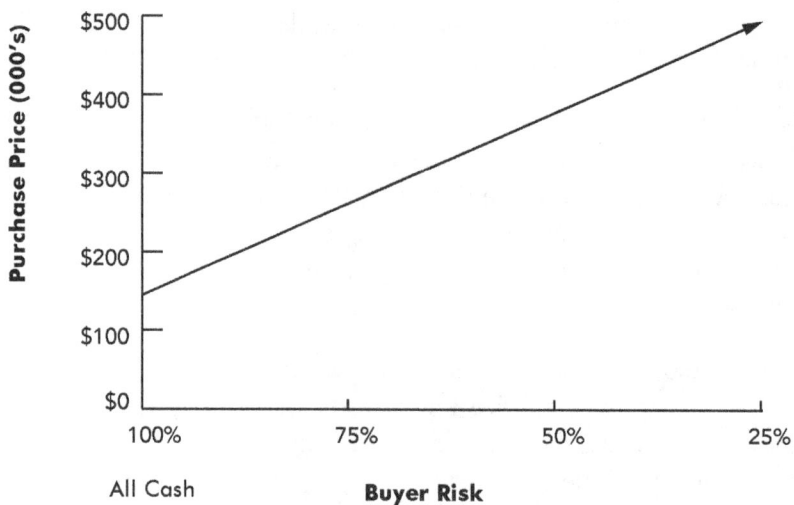

How Much Cash Upfront?

Even in sharing risk, it is usually the seller's desire to get as much cash upfront as possible at closing or soon after. Typical buyers try to minimize the amount of cash outlay.

As a buyer, all of the transition costs, including sign changeover, new marketing materials, moving expenses (if any), kick-off, and public relations expenses, to name a few, will be your responsibility.

The seller may have legitimate needs for cash to settle debts. You may need to assist the buyer with the upfront cash so they can quickly become a productive part of your team. But keep this general rule in mind: The more you are paying upfront or with guaranteed payments, the greater your risk.

And also remember that the more cash upfront the seller receives, the less interest the seller has in the success of the company after closing.

If they get most of their money in year one for example, they may be less likely to help with any issues in year two or three. You are also less protected if an economic slowdown hits. This is why we recommend a fair amount to both sides, typically 20% to 30% cash at closing, and the remaining payments based on the performance of the company in an earn-out over at least three years.

Though sellers may be resistant to longer-term payouts, there are advantages for everyone in deferred payments. To the buyer, there is less financial risk, and it ensures the seller's loyalty and assistance. Deferring payments based on performance also allows most of the future payments (and maybe some profit) to be taken out of the cash flow generated from the acquired agents.

For the seller, in most cases, it can result in tax savings, depending on their tax brackets. If the payments are spread over a number of years, the per-year tax will hopefully be less than if they received all of the purchase price in a lump sum.

The seller will typically ask for a guarantee of the payments. We strongly recommend staying away from any guarantees.

You are guaranteeing to pay the seller the full purchase price based on the agents performing at the level they did when you did your analysis. If the seller will guarantee the future earnings of their agents, then you can guarantee the payment.

We know this does not go over well many times, but the shared-risk strategy is the only way a seller will maximize the potential purchase price. This pricing strategy necessitates the seller believing you will retain the agents, make sound future decisions, and be a good leader for their people.

Negotiating Variables

As you work towards the final price and terms of the transaction, there are a number of basic negotiating variables at your disposal. These can be used to raise or lower the price accordingly.

Depending on the size of the transaction, buyers can use any one of these exclusively, or more typically, they use several variables in some combination. The basic tools include:

- **Cash Upfront:** We recommend this be no more than 20% to 30% of the total purchase price.

- **Pending Sales (0% to 100% of company listing):** Sellers often feel that the pending inventory is theirs to keep and want to retain that income. In reality, the buyer is purchasing 12 months of revenue from the seller. If the buyer does not get the pending inventory, they are receiving only 10 or so months of revenue against 12 months of expenses. On smaller transactions, some buyers will give up a percentage of the company dollar from the pending sales, but this is factored into and counted toward the purchase price. The buyer will have to keep paying the overhead without receiving all the income, so it is fair that pending sales are part of the purchase price.

- **Listings (50% to 100% of company dollar):** This again applies to smaller transactions or folding a few agents into your existing office. As mentioned in our formula section, listings can be the sole basis of a valuation — but they are often used as payments with pending sales, or overrides in small company fold-ins.

- **Sales Agent Or Company Overrides (5% to 20% of company dollar):** At the end of each quarter or the end of the year, the company dollar of each agent is calculated, and the % agreed to is paid to the seller. This is often the only payment method in small transactions of a few agents.

- **Company Dollar/Gross Profit (10% to 20%):** When buying most firms and offices, the purchase price payout will be based off of the company dollar of the firm. Company Dollar/Gross Profit is generally calculated as total revenue minus commissions (often called Cost of Goods Sold), referral fees, and franchise fees. This is essentially what the company has left to pay their normal operating expenses and generate profit with. Payments are made quarterly or annually based on the firm's company dollar. We like to add the provision that the definition of the firm's company dollar is generated only by the production of agents that were with the firm at the time of closing. Payouts are typically over three to four years.

The "Need" Variables

While the above negotiation tools are all essential, they are fairly standard and commonly used. Beyond these, however, you also have certain "need variables" that may tip the scales of a transaction in your favor.

These tend to be particularly helpful tools because they are not used by everybody else. These little-considered variables are why you were encouraged to find out the true motivation and needs of the seller. This allows you to customize a package that not only gets both a fair purchase price but also assists the seller getting to their next chapter as quickly and productively as possible.

Many of these may be more appropriate in smaller transactions, but it might spur your out-of-the-box thinking even in large ones. You may even pay less overall because you have found ways to address the seller's real needs and make the process an easier decision for them.

The following are a few of the specific areas where you can help:

- **Debt Assumption:** As we discussed earlier, if you can help a seller out of a financial crunch, there may be a tremendous benefit for everyone involved. You could assume a portion or all of the debt in lieu of the down payment as a part of the purchase price.

- **Equipment Rental Assumption and Lease Assistance:** When sellers are closing down an office, they are often anxious to get out from under various leases for equipment and the building. Most buyers will make it entirely the seller's responsibility to figure it out. If you can assist, it will be a big plus for you. In acquiring a fold-in that has an existing office to shut down, an approach that has been a very successful strategy for us is to offer to split the lease expenses for up to six months. This consideration is usually not a significant amount of money, but offering to work together with the seller to sub-let the space to another tenant can be a huge advantage for you. This can be a very profitable concession monetarily, and it helps build a new team relationship. It is very beneficial to take away as many impediments that might discourage a seller from saying "yes." Make it as easy as possible to transition to the next chapter, and an office lease can be a deal-breaker.

- **Title/Responsibilities:** Consider making the seller a Vice President or Senior Vice President, or find another appropriate title, even if they are going back into production or only serving in an advisory capacity. This allows the seller to "save face" and feel better about selling the company. The seller can now tell their friends and family they are now a Senior VP with a much larger company. If there is a needed role (whatever it is) they can fill, this is the time to offer it and get them excited about the possibilities.

- **Owner's Commission Split:** If the seller wants to get back to becoming a full-time agent, consider giving them a higher-than-normal split — for example, 80% vs. normal of 70%. Factor what the additional 10% per year will be for three years and apply this to the overall purchase price. They may trust themselves to earn the override back more than the agents.

  If you use this variable, we suggest paying this overage in a separate quarterly check applied to the purchase and not a per-closing one. When the payments stop (earn-out is complete) you want the seller accustomed to a normal split, and this way you will not give the impression of reducing their commission at the conclusion of the payout.

- **Office Space/Administrative Support:** Giving the seller a professional setup at the office for the next year or three will help them transition from being an owner to being an agent or manager. If in production, you may offer to hire administrative support to jump start their activity. It is usually very beneficial to both if you can shift some of the purchase price money into areas that will potentially generate additional revenue to both sides.

- **Insurance Coverage:** This is very much on people's minds these days; if you offer to pick up the seller's family insurance for the next year, that will create a lot of goodwill and reduce family stress. We have in the past estimated the cost and then reduced the purchase offer by 1.5X or more. Providing convenience and reducing seller stress can assist both sides and save you real dollars on the purchase price.

- **Marketing Allowance/ Business Expenses:** This works if the seller goes back into production. It uses a similar concept to the above: Offer to pay them $X per month for their first year. This concept also involves directing portions of the purchase price where it could bring you both back significant returns. It may not be as much fun for the seller as buying a new boat, but it may be the needed investment to get them rolling and productive again.

- **Office Moving Assistance:** This really only applies to a fold-in where you are not taking the existing office. This might seem like a minor thing, but the following is a good example of making it easy on the seller, and it is paying off. We were helping acquire a small company in Florida that was being sold by a retiring seller. Several bidders emerged. None of them wanted her office or furniture. We convinced our buyer in their letter of intent to offer to share the rent for up to six months as we helped sublet the space, to find a buyer for the furniture and give the seller 100% of the furniture proceeds, and to arrange for the cleaning of the office. We knew that the seller had a very fine agent base, but they were ready to sell because they had a sick family member to take care of. We submitted our LOI with what we felt was a very fair offer and got selected over the other bidders. We later learned that our offer was literally tens of thousands less than the others. The seller appreciated the fact that we cared enough to understand their needs, which was much more important to them than maximizing the purchase price. Please do not view this example as taking advantage of anyone; it was still a significant offer and payout, but we took the extra time to determine what would cause the seller to choose *us*. The lesson learned, many times over since then, is that it is not always the most money that secures the transaction in your favor.

We cannot over-emphasize the importance in many transactions of these "need" variables. Do the extra work that most buyers will not do, and you will be rewarded.

But keep in mind that these are not mere "giveaways," designed just to curry favor with the seller and bring the prices down. A smart seller will see through that kind of gimmicky, manipulative approach. You should be trying to invest in the seller's future. You are practicing a win/win approach, trying to find the best short and long-term solutions for both sides.

The interesting thing is that if you manage to determine how best to get the seller to their next chapter, one of the by-products could be a lower price and, more importantly, a successful acquisition.

Having now dealt with all of the many considerations and variables and formulas, you should, at this point, have a sense of how much you want to offer, the structure of the offer, what terms you will propose, and what kind of partnership you wish to create with the seller. All the preparations, at last, are finished.

Now it's time to put the deal in motion and make an offer the seller can't refuse.

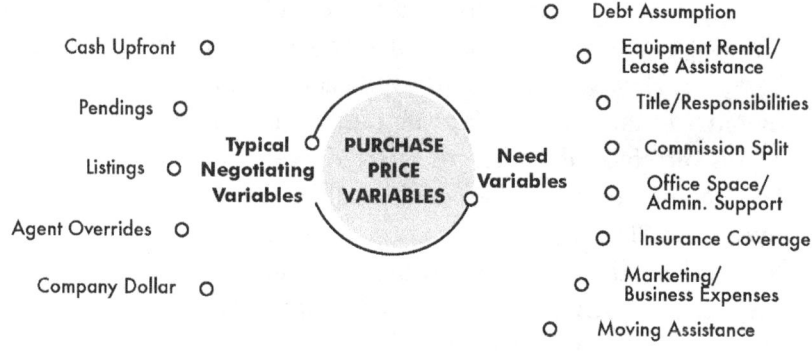

Making The Offer

The excitement builds as you have decided this is an acquisition that can work for you. You have determined how much the seller's firm is worth to you and the terms that would make it most attractive.

Most of the process up until now has comprised fact-finding and informal discussions between you and the seller. Now it is time to actually put an offer on the table.

This is not, however, as easy as tossing out a number; rather, you should now be prepared to present (and sell) a clear and detailed statement of your intentions and your plans for the future of the combined entities (especially the seller's participation in it). Hopefully you have been building the confidence between you and the seller all along, but now it is time to close the deal.

We have talked about developing a vision, and now you must convey that vision and your passion for making it happen in its entirety to the seller. You have researched the seller's needs, motivations, and how best to get them to their next chapter. Now you must prove *you* are the solution, ready and willing to help make their new future a reality.

At the heart of this presentation will be a document known as the Letter of Intent. In this chapter we will cover all of the items that should be included in this important document. But we will also give you tips on how best to present the offer, because this is the point at which the often-misunderstood art of negotiation comes into play.

The Letter Of Intent

At the simplest level, the letter of intent, or LOI, is a written version of all the key points and benefits the seller will derive if they sell to you.

We recommend that the LOI be the first time that you present the proposed terms of the sale to the seller. It should not come as a huge surprise, as it represents a culmination of all the discussions the two of you have had, all the information you have compiled, needs uncovered, and you are negotiating from a mutually agreed foundation on the firm's adjusted EBITDA.

Presenting the LOI is your opportunity to prove that you have listened, provided solutions, and are a partner worth committing to. Every detail of the sale, from the purchase price and terms, down to any assistance with furniture and equipment, their lease, or future roles with the combined companies, must be included.

We do not recommend trying to create a binding LOI. This is a "handshake" agreement between two future partners. If for any reason the seller wants to stop the process at any time up until the closing agreements are signed, we prefer to allow them an exit, never pressuring them into doing something they do not want to do.

We have found that if we are able to get a non-binding LOI signed, there is a very high likelihood of the transaction closing. Because of the way we suggest you approach these negotiations and the need for the cooperation of the seller after closing, it would be culturally wrong to force a close. If there is any "seller's remorse" pre-closing, which we have experienced, we would do everything we can to solve the objections or concerns.

We recommend that the following be addressed in the LOI:

1. **What You Intend To Purchase:** Be detailed and specific. Is it an asset or stock purchase? Is it 100% of the company? Will it include all the furniture and fixtures, lease, assumption of agreements, and so on? Does it include all the pending sales? Does it exclude all the excess cash? Will any operating cash be left in the company? (Sometimes two months or thereabouts is requested.)

2. **The Terms:** Present your offer (the total projected purchase price) and explain how you arrived at the price and terms. This will show the seller how they can best maximize the value and how you plan to recoup your investment. Specify in detail all the terms of the purchase, including the expected payout schedule and how it is calculated (for example: X% of Company Dollar for 3 years). Note whether those payments are conditional based on agent retention, performance, or other variables, and whether they could be greater

or less than the projected purchase price. If it is included, explain to the seller that there will be a "floor and ceiling" in the agreement. This protects the seller in knowing the floor amount is the minimum they will receive, even if the payout has to be extended by a year or two. It also protects the buyer that there is a maximum "premium" that will be paid if the market or the agents have spectacular years.

3. **Other Considerations:** As you have tried to deal with the seller's needs, anything that you have agreed to provide or not provide should be spelled out here. That might include such extras as providing an assistant for six months or a marketing allowance. Will you require agreements to stay from key management or agents?

4. **Non Compete**: We highly recommend you ask for a non-compete agreement from the seller. You can make it part of the purchase price allocated to the non-compete. These are sometimes difficult to enforce, but they are usually upheld through at least the earn-out term.

5. **Diligence Remaining**: Up to this point, the seller may have withheld certain agreements or tax records. Identify what you still need for your verification efforts prior to closing. It is not uncommon to not see the tax returns or certain agreements until after the LOI is signed. You know that you are serious, but often the seller is still not sure and will hold some items they feel are extremely confidential back.

6. **The Agreement:** Specify that the letter is non-binding, so that you and seller have an out if the terms aren't agreeable — or if during the additional diligence you determine the proposed investment isn't appropriate given new information you've uncovered. Disclose that your attorney will draft the closing documents and that each party is responsible for their own legal or advisory fees.

7. **Projected Closing:** Give the projected closing date and location. Depending on the company's size and the complexity of the transaction, it could be as soon as three weeks to as long as three months.

8. **Confidentiality:** Specify that both parties agree to confidentiality regarding the terms or the agreement. We recommend the buyer also include a clause that allows them to control all the public relations and announcements regarding the transaction once

closed. It is always a good idea to coordinate PR efforts because we have seen sellers be the first to tell their friends the news, and then the announcement comes out different than the buyer wanted or it is not the "major splash" that had been planned.

The below sample letter of intent showcases many of the key components we have found necessary for a successful transaction.

SAMPLE Letter of Intent

Between Zebra Realty (buyer) and Sun Realty (seller)

(please secure your own legal advice)

Dear Sally,

This will memorialize our present proposal that, subject to due diligence, the terms and conditions outlined below, and the preparation and execution of definitive written asset purchase agreement and related necessary agreements, Zebra Realty (ZR) intends to acquire all or substantially all of the assets (including pending sales and listings, but excluding cash on hand) of the real estate brokerage and ancillary services of Sun Realty, referred to herein as ("Seller"), for approximately $_____ paid per Schedule "A."

This letter outlines certain terms and conditions precedent of such an acquisition:

1. Completion of all due diligence requested by ZR or its representatives, with results acceptable to ZR.
2. Execution of a definitive asset purchase agreement.
3. Any and all licensing or affiliate agreements of the Seller shall have been terminated and be of no further force or affect, with the termination of any such agreements to have been carried out solely at the volition, and cost, of the Seller, recognizing that ZR has not induced nor advised the Seller to pursue any such efforts.
4. ZR will not assume any debt of the seller. Debt shall include all bank indebtedness, capital leases, non-compete payments, change of control payments, loans to or from former officers or stockholders,

and amounts related to inter-company balances and payments related to the Seller's prior acquisitions or agreements.

5. All terminations and consents necessary or desirable to effect the transactions contemplated hereby shall have been obtained by the Seller solely at the cost of Seller. In addition, any and all agreements of the Seller with related parties or third parties to provide mortgage, title, insurance or other services shall have been terminated and be of no further force of effect unless mutually agreed upon, with the terminations of any such agreements to have been carried out solely at the volition, and cost, of the seller.

6. Under a written agreement not to compete, the seller and all of its shareholders would agree not to compete or solicit for a period of __ years within a __ mile radius of any offices of ZR. *(Remember, this clause is not always enforceable, but it's ideal to have some portion of the purchase price agreed to for the non-compete.)*

7. *(Special circumstances example: Key employee, non-owner)* Whereas Sue Sunshine is a manager and key employee, ZR will engage in negotiations with the assistance of the Seller for an employment/affiliation agreement. As a condition of this transaction, Sue Sunshine shall agree to a non-compete/non-solicitation for similar terms as the shareholders.

8. *(Special circumstances: Agent or team with high % of company GCI)* Whereas Sam Stone and his team are a major part of the value of the firm, seller will assist with the negotiations and, if necessary ensure, out of seller's proceeds that Sam Stone and his team will remain for a minimum of three years.

9. The parties agree to negotiate in good faith the leases at market rent and terms mutually agreed upon for the owned office location (s).

10. The parties shall each pay their own costs and expenses including, without limitation, professional and consulting fees for any and expenses incurred by them in connection with this letter and the transaction contemplated hereby.

11. The seller will pay all operating expenses through the day of closing. Seller will be credited for the amount of any prepaid expenses,

prepaid taxes, and other expenses as adjusted and mutually agreed upon.

12. Other appropriate agreements, documents and instruments, including employment and commission agreements for (the owners), shall have been negotiated and agreed upon. Regardless of the agreement, (the owner) will stay affiliated for a minimum of a three-year period after closing to assist with the transition.

13. Seller covenants and agrees that, from the date hereof to the sooner of the execution of a definitive asset purchase agreement or the Termination Date (as defined below), they and their affiliates will deal exclusively with ZR in connection with the sale or other disposition of all or any of the common stock or assets of the Seller or merger or similar transaction. Seller represents and warrants that no third party has any contractual or legal rights with respect to any sale or other disposition of all or any of the common stock or assets of the Seller or merger or similar transaction.

14. This letter and its provisions herein shall terminate on _____ unless extended in writing by both parties (the "Termination Date").

Except for the provisions of paragraph 13 above, which is intended to be legally binding and enforceable, this letter of intent constitutes only a statement for the intentions of the parties hereto, and it does not contain all matters upon which agreement must be reached for the transaction contemplated hereby to be consummated and is not legally binding on or enforceable against ZR or the Seller.

ACKNOWLEDGEMENT

I have read, understand and agree with the general intentions as hereinabove outlined.

Zebra Realty

Date:

By: John Zebra

_____

Signature and title

Sun Realty

Date:_____

By: Sue Sun

_____

Signature and Title

Schedule "A"

1. Cash at closing to be paid is $_____

2. Estimated additional payments of $_____ will be made as detailed below. Both parties acknowledge the payments may be higher or lower based on the productivity of the agents.

3. One year after the closing and for two additional years (a total of three years), a list of the sales associates who were licensed with Sun Realty (Seller) as of the closing and who are licensed with Zebra Realty as of the end of one year and the following year ends, shall be prepared together with a schedule of their Company Dollar for the one-year time period then ended (the "Post-Closing Company Dollar").

4. Company Dollar shall be defined as gross commission income less all payments made (a) to cooperating brokers, (b) as commissions to sales associates, (c) as Franchise or Network Royalties paid, (d) as referral fees.

5. Post-closing Company Dollar is estimated to be $_____ (*usually use previous 12 months*) and can be adjusted pre-closing as mutually agreed upon.

6. If the Post-Closing Company Dollar is greater than or equal to 95% of the Company Dollar attributable to any of the Seller's sales associates for real estate transactions closed and commissions paid

during the years one through six time periods (or shorter), then Zebra Realty shall pay Seller __% of the Company Dollar and years one through three.

7. If the Post-Closing Company Dollar is greater than 85%, but is less than 95%, of the Company Dollar attributable to any of the Seller's sales associates for real estate transactions closed and commissions paid during the years one through five time periods, then ZR shall pay Seller an amount between 0% and __% of the Company Dollar based on the actual percentage of Post-Closing Company Dollar to Pre-Closing Company Dollar (For example, if Post –Closing Company Dollar is equal to 90%, then ZR shall pay to seller ____ of the time periods Company Dollar (90% X __%).

8. If the Post-Closing Company Dollar is less than or equal 85% of the Pre-Closing Company Dollar, no additional payments shall be made for that one-year time period. (Note: You want to have the ability as a buyer to stop payment if there is a plunge in revenue from the sellers agents)

9. During year one, the seller will be paid a total transitional salary of $_____. Seller will be responsible for the normal business and personal expenses as these were added back to the profit calculation. (Note: This may be a good option if you have specific duties for the seller.)

Stock vs. Asset Purchases

In a stock purchase, the buyer acquires the target company's stock, which represents ownership in the company. In an asset purchase, the buyer acquires specific assets of the target company, such as real estate, intellectual property, or equipment.

There are several key differences between stock purchases and asset purchases:

1. **Legal structure:** In a stock purchase, the legal structure of the target company remains unchanged, and the company continues to operate under the same legal entity. In an asset purchase, the

target company may be dissolved or restructured, and the assets are transferred to the buyer.

2. **Liabilities:** In a stock purchase, the buyer assumes all of the target company's liabilities, including any debts or legal obligations. In an asset purchase, the buyer only assumes the liabilities associated with the specific assets being acquired.

3. **Tax implications:** The tax implications of a stock purchase and an asset purchase can differ, depending on the specific circumstances of the transaction. It is important to carefully consider the tax implications of each type of purchase.

4. **Due diligence:** In a stock purchase, the buyer typically performs due diligence on the target company as a whole, including its financial and operational condition. In an asset purchase, the buyer may focus on the specific assets being acquired and may not need to perform as comprehensive due diligence.

Overall, the decision to pursue a stock purchase or an asset purchase will depend on the specific circumstances of the transaction and the goals of the parties involved. It is important to carefully consider the pros and cons of each type of purchase and to seek the advice of legal and financial advisors.

Asset vs. Stock Sale

We always recommend that you get your own legal and tax advice prior to buying or selling a real estate company. As we are all too well aware, the federal and state tax laws, tax percentages, and benefits can and do change often. Please do not rely on what could be incorrect or outdated information.

However, we would be remiss in not presenting the concept and differences of an asset vs. a stock sale. Based on our current knowledge, and the fact that we are not tax experts, we believe the following to be correct.

The decision of which structure is best is complicated by the fact that the buyer and seller usually benefit most from opposing structures. Generally, buyers prefer asset sales, while sellers prefer stock sales.

As a recap, an asset sale (in theory) purchases only specific assets and liabilities of the seller. There can be situations where some prior misdeed by the seller could cause the buyer to be dragged into a lawsuit, but in an asset sale, the buyer is much more insulated.

In a stock sale, the buyer purchases the seller's shares in the corporation — and, in theory, also inherits all the good and bad that transfer with those shares. There are obviously representations and warrants that we recommend being added to the agreement for protection, but in practice buying stock is more risky from a future litigation perspective.

While there are many considerations when negotiating a purchase and sale, potential liabilities and tax implications are of primary concern.

It should be noted that if a business is a sole proprietorship, partnership, or the popular limited liability corporation (LLC), a transaction cannot be structured as a stock sale because none of these forms of ownership have stock. They can, however, sell their partnership of membership interest as opposed to the entity selling its assets. If the business is a regular C-corporation, or a sub-S, then that transaction can be structured as either a stock or asset sale.

To complicate the decision even more, the current Internal Revenue Code allows buyers and sellers of the stock of an S-corporation to make a Section 338(h)(10) election so that a qualified stock purchase will be treated as a deemed asset purchase for federal income tax purposes.

A Section 338(h)(10) election is a joint election that requires agreement between and among all of the selling shareholders and the prospective buyer. As a result of this election, a stock sale for legal purposes will be treated as an asset sale for tax purposes, resulting in different tax consequences for both the buyer and seller that selling shareholders need to understand.

Importantly, a Section 338(h)(10) election will adjust the tax basis of the S-corporation's assets in the hands of the buyer to fair-market value. The buyer may enjoy incremental tax benefits as a result, including amortization and depreciation of the assets' purchase price for federal income tax purposes, along with resulting future tax deductions for the amount paid over the tax life of the acquired assets.

Buyers typically prefer asset sales not only for future liability consideration, but also for tax purposes. Current IRS guidelines allow buyers to "step-up" the company's depreciable basis in its assets. By allocating a higher value for assets that depreciate quickly, such as equipment, and allocating a lower value to assets that amortize slowly, such as goodwill, the buyer gains additional tax benefits.

Sellers typically want to have as much allocated to goodwill as possible, rather than to hard assets. This can be the difference in paying higher ordinary income rates on the hard assets vs. capital gains rates on the goodwill. For sellers, there is also a risk of double taxation if the entity is a C-corporation. Of course, each individual's tax situation is unique.

With a stock sale, buyers lose the ability to gain a stepped-up basis in the assets. The basis of the assets at the time of sale (book value) sets the depreciation basis for the buyer, which can result in higher future taxes.

Fortunately for both sides, the amount of hard assets (for example, furniture and fixtures) in most transactions is small compared to the overall purchase price. Sellers favor stock transactions primarily because all of the purchase price proceeds are taxed at lower capital gains rates. Stock sales also allow C-corporation sellers to bypass the corporate level taxes.

With all the above being true, still almost every small and medium M&A real estate brokerage transaction is an asset sale. Usually, the buyer and seller's accountants can work together to find a fair balance for the allocation of the assets purchased vs. the goodwill. (Remember: Please always get your own legal and tax advice.)

What is Goodwill in a Real Estate Acquisition?

Goodwill is an intangible asset that represents the positive reputation and image of a company. It is the value that a company has built up over time in the eyes of its customers, employees, shareholders, and the broader community.

Goodwill is typically associated with a company's brand, customer loyalty, and the positive relationships that it has cultivated with its stakeholders.

Goodwill can be a valuable asset for a company, as it can contribute to customer loyalty, employee retention, agent retention, and overall business success. For example, if a company has a strong reputation for ethical behavior and high-quality real estate transactions, it may be able to gain market share because customers are more likely to work with the firm based on the trust and confidence that they have developed.

However, goodwill can also be at risk if a company engages in activities that damage its reputation or harm its relationships with stakeholders. For example, if a company is involved in a scandal or is perceived as behaving unethically, it could suffer significant harm to its goodwill and reputation, which could ultimately impact its financial performance.

In negotiating transactions, the seller will often tout that their firm has been in business for 50+ years and they are the best name in the area. They will request a premium on the multiple because of that fact.

Obviously, it is always better to acquire a firm with a strong reputation than a lesser one. Goodwill is a part of the multiple calculation process; however, goodwill is also reflected in the adjusted EBITDA. With their 50 years in business how much EBITDA were they able to produce?

We have seen many real estate companies that are worth more in five years than the local decades-old brokerage because of the quality agents they recruited and the growth they were able to create. The bottom line is that positive goodwill is important, but it must be reflected in earnings to be greatly beneficial.

Goodwill is typically calculated on a company's balance sheet as an intangible asset and the excess of the purchase price of a business over the fair-market value of its tangible assets and liabilities. This excess is referred to as the "purchase price premium," and it is used to determine the value of the goodwill on the balance sheet.

For example, if a company purchases another business for $10 million and the fair-market value of the tangible assets and liabilities of the business is $8 million, the purchase price premium would be $2 million. This $2 million would be recorded as goodwill on the company's balance sheet.

There are several methods that can be used to determine the fair-market value of a company's tangible assets and liabilities, including the market approach, the income approach, and the cost approach.

The market approach involves comparing the company being purchased to similar companies that have been sold recently, while the income approach involves estimating the future cash flows that the company is expected to generate and discounting it back to present value. The cost approach involves estimating the cost to replace the company's tangible assets and liabilities.

It is important to note that goodwill is considered to be an intangible asset, and it is not subject to depreciation. Instead, it is tested for impairment on an annual basis, and any impairment loss is recorded as a charge against earnings. If the value of goodwill decreases, it may be necessary to write down the value of the asset on the balance sheet.

The Presentation: Problem-Solving Time

Once you've developed a letter of intent, either in a rough or finished form, how do you present it to the seller? This is, in effect, your "problem-solving meeting," where you are sharing with the seller the solutions you have developed to the various problems and needs of all the parties involved.

We prefer to present the vision and deal points *before* we give the LOI to the seller. It is just normal behavior that the seller will go straight to read the purchase price and maybe the terms, start thinking about those items, and not hear any more of your conversation.

Everyone has their own preferred style, but we like to get all the benefits on the table before getting into the specifics of the numbers.

The meeting and LOI should be presented to the seller not just as an offer, but as a blueprint for the future. You should make it clear that the particular needs of the seller — for example, the desire to become an agent again, retire, or pursue other aspirations — have been carefully considered and incorporated into the proposal.

On larger transactions, we always have a completed LOI that we walk the potential sellers through after we present the benefits and vision of the combined companies. This is typically a more formal meeting. It really depends on your personal preferences and style.

On smaller transactions, we prefer to be less formal, and we might say, "We are putting together our formal offer, but first we would like to tell you what we are thinking and get your impressions." This approach can be viewed as more collaborative, and it may also allow you to uncover any real negative attitudes on a type of payment variable you are considering.

Regardless of a formal or informal strategy, this meeting should:

- **Reinforce the new company vision.** Discuss the potential, where can we both go together. How as partners (in spirit) you will all be able to go further than separately. Talk about how you have taken the best interests of the seller, their family, agents, employees, and clients into consideration. Present a view of how the seller fits with the new company, or how this offer will accelerate their ability to do what they really would prefer doing.

- **Soothe concerns.** Create a situation where the transition looks achievable and not too painful by making it clear that you understand, empathize with, and have addressed potential problems such as leases, debts, or anything that might make it more difficult for a seller to say "yes." Plan for the "What would I do about _____?" or the "How would it work?" questions that will be asked.

- **Articulate the offer.** Show the seller the estimated total purchase price, when the payments will occur, and what they will be based on. An example for a small company you are folding in might be 20% of the project purchase price at closing, 30% over the next 90 days, based on 50% of the company dollar as close, and 15% of your agent's company dollar for the next two years, estimated to be $X. Point out the items you have included to help the seller with their new career or next chapter.

- **Communicate that this is a serious offer** that you have spent much deliberation over, one that is fair and that incorporates the needs and maximizes the value to both sides. You have spent a great deal of time and energy looking at the best way to go forward. The financial and cultural considerations must be right for both parties for the transaction to be successful. You are not presenting a lowball or first offer as a negotiating ploy (even if the seller feels it is low). You want to establish right away that you are open to discussion and you want to find mutual solutions, but you are making what you believe to be your best offer that would work to maximize the benefit to both.

For this approach to work, you must really start out with your best offer (or close to it), as opposed to an unrealistically low one. We would always come in a little low, maybe 10% to 15% below our final "walk away" price. We needed to convey to the seller we were serious, but we also allowed a little victory for the seller in the negotiations.

If you come in too low, it could result in the seller not even countering, losing trust in the relationship — and once this kind of win-lose negotiation process gets started, it is hard to stop, and you will probably lose either money or the transaction in the process.

It is natural for the seller to want to put forth a counter-offer, and this should be expected, but you must convey clearly that even though you really want this to work, you are getting very close to the total amount you can reasonably justify, and this is not a bidding process you are intending but a carefully considered and constructed offer designed to best meet everyone's needs.

If a counter-offer is proposed, then go back to your valuation premise. A restructuring of the terms could provide for a potentially higher price, or using a different variable may be more appealing to the seller. There are usually a number of acceptable ways to structure a transaction while still making it financially feasible.

PRESENTING THE OFFER

When presenting the offer you must:

a. Reinforce the new company vision
b. Satisfy as many needs of the seller as possible
c. Communicate how you will assist the seller get to their next chapter
d. Express the win-win approach and why it is important
e. Make it clear that your offer is fair and why
f. Be able to answer the "what if" questions
g. Expect a "no" or "this won't work"
h. Try to understand what the possible solutions are
i. Be willing to walk away

Often it is a best practice to present a preliminary transition plan at this meeting to assure the seller: 1) you really are prepared and thorough; 2) the agents and clients will be taken care of in a professional manner and there will be direction; and 3) if the seller says "yes," this will really happen, be done well, not take too much work, and be over with soon.

This conversation also begins a very nice "assumptive close" process. Working on details of the transition plan together means that the seller is beginning to visualize this transaction occurring.

Chapter 7: Pre-Closing

The Transition Plan

The period between the signing of the LOI and up to a few weeks (depending on size) before closing is the time to develop and coordinate a transition plan, in which you identify all the activities that must be accomplished prior to closin

Hopefully, you begin talking with the seller about the transition either before or immediately after you have a signed LOI. You should make it clear that as you move forward to the signing of the contract and beyond, you will need the seller's help every step of the way.

It is a good time to ask for advice — for example, "How should we best communicate this to your key employees and agents, and how might the announcement meeting be handled?" The two (or more) of you will be working closely to ensure all aspects of the pre- and post-announcement and integration run smoothly.

Some buyers may want to wait until they know the transaction will close before ordering new signs, or materials for the new agents. There will be some financial risk if it does not close, but it is more of a financial risk if the transaction closes and the materials that the new agents need are not ready in hour one.

The transition plan is designed to maximize the retention and minimize any lost productivity due to confusion, missing materials, or lack of direction. All of these troublesome issues will cause breakage, and we speak from experience.

As soon as the merger announcement is made, competitors will be calling on the agents and offering new options. Your job is to make the transition as easy, positive, and seamless for the agents. You want it so well done that the new agents are complimenting the professionalism, planning, and the difference they already feel with the new company.

The goal is to create minimal "down-time," allowing them to go out and secure new business the afternoon of the announcement, under the new company — not days later.

Remember, you and the seller have been working on this transaction for weeks or months. For your staff and agents, they are on day one. A well-planned transition is the most critical step to reduce any potential breakage.

The transition plan should include the following:

- **Transition Team:** Who is going to be on the transition team? Depending on the size of the transaction and the trust in the people, it is best to have a few people on the team from each firm. It may be only the seller and buyer but in larger transactions we have worked with up to 8 to 10 people on the committee. This is where a project code name is important in addition to sworn confidentiality.

- **Activities Identified:** What needs to be done, by whom, and by when, and the top-level person responsible. Some buyers actually prepare shares.

- **Major Events:** Get working immediately on the venues, dates, and times for the major events that you want to occur, such as: the key stakeholder dinner, agent kick-off meeting, and any industry or community impact events.

- **Momentum Multiplier:** What internal and external activities can be conducted or created that will use the excitement of the merger to accelerate our business? Are there recruiting opportunities that this announcement will open up, or even other acquisition candidates? Use the first 90 days after close to exponentially increase your business.

- **Budget Prepared:** Consider how much it will cost to transition the company; it can be a substantial expense that people often underestimate or overlook completely. There can be a big cash outlay for signs, marketing materials, lock boxes, and items with outdated logos thats an agent might have. All of the new people must be converted into your culture and adopt your brand, and it should not cost them any money. Imagine if a new agent had recently ordered 50 rider signs with their name on it in the previous company's colors. You want them to use the new branding, and so you will probably have to buy them new rider signs, or risk causing some malcontent. Budget for these unusual but common occurrences.

- **Materials Ordered:** Business cards, name badges, signs, and so on should be ready for the kick-off day (which is usually the day after closing). New agents will be impressed when you hand them a complete gift-wrapped kit at the kick-off meeting, ready for them to go to work.

- **Communicating To The Agents:** One of the very first things, and probably the most important to your success, will be deciding when to bring in any key stakeholders to the news. Most buyers and sellers like to control the timing and content of the announcement closely as opposed to telling some of the key agents too early, and the news leaking out early, as it almost always does. This can cause much more concern and speculation on the agent's parts who may be hearing the news a little distorted and "third hand." We have also been involved in the other extreme, where all (or a select few) agents are aware of the negotiations and are a part of the decision and blessing of the transaction.

Typically, top-producing agents and key stakeholders will be told of the "merger" the night before the rest of the company is told at an exclusive event, such as a private dinner or reception. A format we have used would have the seller meet with their people for a half hour or so, explaining what is happening, before the buyer arrives and talks about the benefits of the combined entities. We have also had successful events where the seller and buyer together present the exciting news of the merger and associated benefits to all.

We have even used a top agent from the buyer's company to successfully share the advantages they are about to enjoy.

The seller must ask their agents to trust the decision and that the best interests of the agents have been carefully considered. As company leaders, the other agents will look to this group for the "thumbs up or down" sign. The seller has hopefully earned the right to ask for their support, or for a minimum of a "wait and see" attitude if they cannot be positively supportive. Both you and the seller should ask: "If there are any concerns, please reserve judgment for 60 days. Give us a chance to prove to you the benefits we have worked so hard to put together.

- **First 90 Days Planned:** This would identify the dates and times that you will be conducting the orientation and onboarding program for the new agents, including any training on the brand, marketing programs, internal logistics, tools, or systems. You will want to establish one-on-one reviews and counseling sessions for all new agents.
- **Office Policies and Procedures:** Evaluate both companies and choose the best of the two worlds, then determine how to implement and communicate effectively to both new and existing agents.
- **New Company Business Plan and Pro Forma:** It is time to take the rough pro forma created earlier and fine-tune it. Create the worst-case, best-case and most likely scenarios for a minimum of one year, but preferably two to three.

As you can see, the transition plan can be fairly elaborate, though it should be noted that the plan usually varies based on the size and expense of the acquisition. Obviously, it is easier to absorb five people than fifty, but most of the advice and components apply to both scenarios, just on a different scale. In any case, it is important to get started on the transition plan early, get the help you need, involve the seller, and be prepared for the news to escape early. What is the messaging you and the seller agree on if that happens?

With the LOI signed and your transition plan underway, the acquisition is now almost complete. But this is not time to relax. As the excitement of the impending transaction picks up, it is important to keep moving forward,

and as quickly as possible, to the final stages of closing the deal and signing the contract.

Acquisition Checklist

There is some overlap between a transition plan and a pre-closing checklist.

In theory, the transition plan is part of the pre-closing check-list and covers at least the first 90 days post-closing. As we discussed earlier, the outline of the transition plan is often presented at or near the LOI presentation as an additional closing tool in the transaction. The pre-closing checklist outline (not necessarily filled in) could also be presented to demonstrate that once the LOI is signed, you as the buyer will have a coordinated plan to ensure as smooth and seamless of a transition as possible.

Hopefully, both of these well-thought-out checklists are an aid in assuring the buyer that they are in very capable hands.

We have worked with firms with checklists just a couple of pages long, literally written on a yellow pad, up to large firms with literally dozens of pages and 100+ items to complete prior to or shortly after closing. We would recommend *not* showing an extremely long document to the sellers at the LOI presentation, as it could also be overwhelming, but share a few pages to show your ability to close this transaction in a positive manner.

The following is just a sample of a checklist. In our additional offering, *Acquiring Profit Implementation System*, we have a multi-page digital example that you can modify to your needs.

Buyer's Sample Pre-Closing Acquisition Checklist

(A More Compete Checklist Available in The Acquiring Profit Implementation System)

*Acquired Company   (Announcement/Kick-off 1 day after closing or closing + 1 days)   (Days)

Function	Type	Item/Project	Task Description	Lead Time	Deadline for Completion
Facilities	Signage	Exterior Signage	Arrange for replacement of exterior building signage	-45	closing +1
Facilities	Signage	Interior Signage	Arrange for replacement of interior building signage	-42	closing +1
Facilities	Request Docs-* AC	Bldg./Equip. Leases	Obtain all leases, review, negotiate,	-30	closing -7
Purchasing/Mktg	Request docs- AC	Yard Signs	Obtain special market signage need (condo, lots, commerc.)	-40	closing -2
Purchasing/Mktg	Request docs	Banners	Order banners (New Company name, we've moved, etc.)	-40	closing -2
Purchasing/Mktg	Request info- AC	Sign Installation	Obtain list of sign installers if needed and arrange replacement	-30	closing -7
Marketing	Meetings & Events	Kickoff Event	Schedule Kickoff and subsequent meetings	-45	closing -7
Marketing	Advertising	Announcements	Create acquisition announcements for media	-15	closing -1
Marketing	Advertising	Budget	Establish promotion/marketing budget	-45	closing -30
Administration	Request docs- AC	Procedure Manuals	Obtain and review all policy and procedure manuals	-30	closing -14
Administration	Request docs- AC	Listing/Sales Info	Obtain samples of entry sheets for conversion to our system	-30	closing -7
Administration	Licenses & Boards	Change broker code	Notify local Board(s) asking broker code switched	-15	closing -0
Human Resources	Request docs- AC	Payroll Register	Obtain most current payroll register and set-up internally	-14	closing -2
Human Resources	General	HR Packets	Determine what included, create sales assoc. new hire packets	-21	closing -2
Human Resources	Request docs- AC	Sales Assoc Info	Obtain and SA partnerships, corporations, team info, etc.	-21	closing -2
Accounting	General	Comm. Disbursements	Determine procedures until taken internally	-21	closing -7
Accounting	Request docs- AC	Commission Schedules	Enter Sales Associate (SA) schedules into internal system	-14	closing -2
Accounting	Request docs- AC	Branch Mgr. Comp	Identify and enter internally comp policy and calculations	-14	closing -2
IT	General	Transition	Change logos on intranet and internet sites	-14	closing +1
IT	Training	Intranet Training	Distribute training materials to admins and mgrs.	-7	closing +1
IT	Request docs- AC	Email	obtain current email addresses for all agents and staff	-7	closing +1
Training	Mtgs & Events	Training Needs	Prepare presentation/materials for Kickoff & Orientation	-14	closing -4
Training	Mtgs & Events	Existing Calendar	Review current training calendar and expand where necessary	-14	closing -4
Training	Mtgs & Events	Training Needs	Determine locations/times for orientation and add'l events	-14	closing -4
Sr. Management	General	Closures/mergers	Analyze potential office closures, staff reassignment	-21	closing -7
Sr. Management	General	Transition	Identify potential transition team members	-14	closing +1
Sr. Management	Contracts	Employ. Agreements	Review to determine status, modification needs	-14	closing -4

We completely understand that many of you do not have a huge staff to assist in this endeavor. You may not have divisions or departments to take care of their appropriate tasks. In fact, it may be only the owner and one or two others who also have full-time duties to assist.

Both the transition plan and the pre-closing checklist can be modified into smaller versions with just the essentials by following our example. We strongly recommend that if this is your first acquisition, or if you have never recorded and documented your previous plans, to do so on this acquisition. It may seem like extra work, but it will pay you back many times over in future acquisitions.

We work with many clients, and it is extremely rare to find a company that has done only one acquisition in the past and then stopped. Each subsequent acquisition gets easier, with your techniques and processes improving. Please assume that your first acquisition will not be your last, and plan accordingly.

The time period between the definitive purchase agreement being signed and the closing is a great time to get your transition team started. At this point, it may only include members of your own management team, key staff, and trustworthy agents. You can and should add members of the acquired company post-closing. During this pre-close period, it also might be helpful to have the seller(s) involved as members of the transition team.

Before divulging the name of the acquired company, it is a good idea to get individual NDAs signed. They all should be covered under your original NDA with the prospect, but we like to show the importance of their confidentiality and the potential harm a leak may cause to both sides.

We usually recommend choosing a few agents who are influencers but not necessarily top producers. These sessions can even help bring your team closer together and better aligned.

The transition team should be charged with helping to create plans for:

1. The Kick-off Day Agenda & Activities
2. Welcome Reception/Event
3. Frequently Asked Question Preparation
4. Community Impact Day
5. Integration of New Agents

6. Maximizing The Momentum: New Listing, Buyers, Recruits
7. Dealing With Issues/Conflicts That May Arise

The Contract

Some who are embarking on their first acquisition may feel more comfortable hiring an attorney to create a contract for them. Our advice is: Be very careful around the selection of the attorney. Get a recommendation from a fellow broker (or us) for an attorney who is familiar with M&A, and specifically M&A transactions in the real estate brokerage world.

Just as we would not advise hiring a CPA who is not familiar with real estate firms to value your company, an attorney without prior experience can be a very expensive learning lesson on both sides. An unqualified attorney may only use a "boilerplate" agreement downloaded from their contract service and might not understand the nuances of a real estate brokerage acquisition. They can also charge as little as $10,000 for a small transaction to well over $50,000 for larger ones.

We do not intend to disparage all attorneys, as an experienced M&A one can be invaluable to a successful transaction. Our advice is to lean on others for recommendations and to do your homework to find the right one for you.

We provide a sample of what should be included in agreement and even a sample agreement in the Acquiring Profit Implementation System. This may be a good starting point to give to an attorney unfamiliar with the intricacies of real estate, and it can also save you quite a bit of time, money, and heartache.

Once you are comfortable with your contract, it can then be the basis for your future acquisitions.

The Definitive Purchase Agreement

We always recommend a two-step process to close the transaction, utilizing a Definitive Purchase Agreement, or DPA, prior to the actual closing.

A DPA can be used with an asset or stock sale. It transfers ownership of a business and its assets. The advantages are numerous for both the buyer and the seller.

The DPA is the final agreement that is signed between the seller and buyer, replacing the letter of intent or offer to purchase. The DPA is signed before the closing and the change in possession of the assets or company.

Even if a DPA is signed prior to closing, there can still be contingencies inserted, such as the approval of the franchise or brand, or the need to get a signature on a lease assignment. The sale is automatically canceled if the contingencies are not satisfied before closing, unless mutually extended.

A DPA sets the date for completing the sale through a closing. On the closing date, the buyer will acknowledge that all the contingencies have been satisfied and deliver the agreed-upon down payment, if any. The seller signs and delivers the closing documents, and most importantly, signs documents stating that there has been no material change to the business since the DPA was signed.

The primary advantage of a two-step approach is certainty for both the buyer and seller. The seller may be worried about whether this transaction will actually happen and will not want to spend a lot of time planning the transition, giving access to staff or facilities pre-closing, or even need to see all the representations and warrants that the buyer will request in an agreement.

Similar issues can be true for a buyer. We have worked with clients who invested large amounts of time and money following the LOI, only to have the transaction fall out between the LOI and the closing. Many times the LOI misses a few things that are really important to the buyer or seller, which does not surface until the closing documents are prepared.

Our goal has always been to get a DPA to the seller as quickly as possible to avoid any issues that might arise down the road. We have a few clients who will not invest in any transition expenses or get too far down the planning process until the DPA is signed.

In most cases, there is a 30-day timeframe between the two events. This is often enough to go full speed by both parties to order transition materials and plan and execute on the pre-acquisition checklist and transition plan. Both sides now know with much more certainty that the transaction is happening, unless a material change or contingency is not met. Obviously, the larger the transaction, the more financially the buyer is at risk if the closing falls through.

Even in smaller transactions, we recommend the DPA and the closing. We find that the transactions just run smoother, and it is easier to plan and work in cooperation with the seller. With a closing date well into the future, the planned kick-off or announcements are usually planned for the day after the final closing, just to allow time to fix any last-minute contingency issues.

Below are some of the most important basic components that should be in any contract (either asset or stock):

- **What are you buying, and how are you paying for it?** Spell out very specifically what you are purchasing (furniture, fixtures, goodwill, pending sales, listings, and so on) and how you are going to pay for it (dates and amounts of deferred payments), just as you did in the letter of intent. Any terms should be explained in detail.

  It is also a good idea to apply specific dollar amounts of the purchase price toward specific assets, such as furniture and fixtures, goodwill, and the non-compete agreement. Your tax advisor will assist in this process, but often it is a compromise with the seller as what is a better tax advantage for the buyer can mean the opposite for the buyer.

- **Publicity:** It is very important to specify that the buyer has total responsibility and authority to handle any communications with the outside world and the press. We have seen acquisitions in which the seller, not the buyer, handled the publicity, and ended up distorting the information, making it look as if the seller's company was the acquirer and was going to trim back the management staff.

- **Websites and Phone Numbers:** Make sure you document the web addresses and websites you will be acquiring. You may want to redirect them, and also it's important to not let the domains expire and get picked up by a competitor. Office phone numbers are also items you want to acquire and have control over going forward. Do not assume; document these and any other critical marketing tools or agreements.

- **Make Sure Investigations Survive The Closing:** If you find out after close that the seller knowingly or unwittingly misled you about anything, you will want the right to adjust the contract, and subsequently the payment amount, accordingly.

- **Non-Compete Agreement And Executive Retention:** These may not be enforceable, but you want to include them anyway and put the parties on notice. Many are enforceable if the parties acknowledge that part of the purchase price is paid as compensation for the non-compete agreement.

- **Ability To Own and Dispense With The Company Name:** You want to own the rights to the seller's company name. Even if you are not going to use that name, then it should be specified that the name can no longer be used in any capacity. The seller's company can remain an active corporation that you can pay money to through the length of the payout, but it cannot operate again in real estate or any other business.

- **Confidentiality:** Once more, we deal with the matter of confidentiality; this time, the seller and buyer agree that they will not disclose any particulars contained in the agreement (such as how much was paid and how). This clause is designed to protect the next transaction you might negotiate differently.

- **Seller Cannot Assign Income:** This is another critical clause. In a traditional asset acquisition agreement or stock sale, the seller can assign future income to a third party, such as a company that buys future earnings at a discounted rate. But unless mutually agreed to, you typically do not want this to happen. Part of the reason you are giving the seller future earnings is to retain loyalty. You do not want the seller to have the ability to cash out to an accounts-receivable company; you want the seller to stick around to support your mutual efforts as an interested party.

- **No Material Changes:** You want assurances from the seller that there has not been any significant events that would alter the underlying numbers used in your valuation of the company. Examples would be a top agent or staff member leaving prior to closing, or a lawsuit that had not been disclosed previously.

Sample Asset Purchase Agreement

Seek legal counsel; do not use this agreement without advisement

THIS AGREEMENT is made as of the _____ day of _____, _____, between _____, a _____ corporation ("Seller"); and _____, a _____ corporation of their assigns as permitted herein (Buyer"); and_____, sole shareholder of Seller ("Shareholder").

In consideration of the premises and the mutual covenants and agreements herein contained, the parties agree as follows:

1. *Transfer of Assets*. On the closing Date hereinafter defined, Seller will convey to Buyer by Bill of Sale and Buyer will purchase and acquire all of the Seller's right. title and interest in and to the following assets of Seller (the "Transferred Assets"): all of Seller's pending contracts, listing agreements, telephone numbers, website, domain names, furniture, fixtures, and equipment listed on the attached Exhibit A; and goodwill. All assets not listed above are not being transferred hereunder. Buyer will assume no liabilities of Seller, except the lease between Landlord, Inc. and Seller on attached Exhibit B and the lease between ABC office Systems and Seller on attached Exhibit C. (*Sellers sometimes ask to have the acknowledgement of the exclusion of the company's cash from the purchase included)*

2. *Purchase Price.* The total consideration to be paid by Buyer for the Transferred Assets shall be estimated at $500,000 (the "Purchase Price") paid as follows: $100,000 cash at closing, and 15% of the Company Dollar generated by the agents of the seller's company at the time of closing for a period of three (3) years or four (4) years if a minimum additional payment of $250,000 has not been met by the end of year three (3). Additional purchase price payments will be made within fifteen (15) days of the end of the calendar year. Seller will have the right to audit the payment calculations annually. (*Sometimes this is included in an Exhibit with sample calculations, especially if there are thresholds and multiple payment mechanisms built in.*)

3. *Instruments of Transfer.* The sales, assignment, and deliveries to be made to Buyer pursuant hereto shall be effected by the Bill of Sale, attached hereto as Exhibit E. Any time and from time to time after the closing date, on Buyer's request, Seller will execute, acknowledge, and deliver all such assignments, and transfers, as may be reasonably required in conformity with this Agreement for the adequate assigning or transferring to Buyer of the Assets sold to Buyer provided herein.

4. *Closing.* The Closing of the sale and transfer contemplated by this Agreement shall take place at the office of Buyer's attorney at _____p.m. on _____, _____. Time is of the essence. All revenue and company expenses incurred prior to closing shall be to the benefit or the responsibility of the Seller. All revenue and expenses shall be the Buyer's responsibility from Closing Date onward. Expenses will be prorated and both parties agree to either paying or receiving additional funds during an expense "true-up" date 30 days hence.

5. *Legal, Accounting and Brokerage Fees.* Each party will bear its own expenses and fees incurred in connection with the transaction contemplated hereby, including without limitation, fees and expenses of accountants and attorneys.

6. *Warranties and Representations.* Seller hereby warrants and represents to Buyer, as of the date hereof and as of the Closing Date, as follows:

a. Seller has good and marketable title to, and owns, the Transferred Assets to be sold, assigned, and transferred hereunder, and the Transferred Assets shall be transferred to the Buyer free and clear from any and all judgements, mortgages, pledges, liens, leases, security interest, options, or other encumbrances or claims, except for the listing inventory, which must be approved by each property owner. *(The listing inventory sometimes transfers, too.)*

b. Seller possesses all necessary power to enter into this Agreement and to consummate the transactions contemplated hereby; the execution and delivery of this agreement has been duly authorized by the sole shareholder of Seller.

c. Pending closing, Seller will conduct business in the ordinary course and use best efforts to preserve relationships with clients and Seller's reputation with agents and in the community; Buyer and Buyer's representatives will be allowed reasonable access during agreed upon times; Seller will furnish such information concerning the business as Buyer may reasonably request.

d. Seller knows of no development which would materially and adversely affect the business.

Buyer hereby represents to the Seller, as of the Closing Date, that: Buyer possesses all necessary power and authority to enter into this Agreement to consummate the transaction contemplated hereby.

a. All information provided by the Seller will be kept in strict confidence by Buyer except for:

(i) Disclosures to attorneys, accountants, and financial advisors of Buyer provided they fall under the terms of the NDA dated _____, or approved by Seller.

(ii) Disclosures compelled by legal process.

7. *Assignment.* Buyer may assign this agreement to an entity formed and owned by Buyer, but such assignment shall not relieve Buyer from personal liability for compliance with the terms and conditions of this agreement.

8. *Covenant not to Compete: Cooperation.* The Seller agrees for a period of three (3) years from the Date of Closing that she will keep her real estate license with _____ and will not, directly or indirectly, as owner, partner, employee, consultant, or otherwise, own a real estate services company, or sell or list real estate with any other company within 30 miles of any of the Buyer's offices. The Buyer agrees to pay a commission split of _____. Seller acknowledges that 25% of the Purchase Price has been paid as compensation for this non-compete provision.

9. *General Provisions.* This agreement shall be executed, construed and performed in accordance with the laws of the State of _____. This Agreement constitutes the entire agreement among the parties pertaining to its subject matter and supersedes all prior and contemporaneous negotiations, agreements, and understandings, written or oral, or the parties connection with it. No representation, covenant, or condition not expressed in this Agreement shall affect, change or restrict this Agreement. Words used herein in the singular shall include the plural and words in the masculine shall include words in the feminine or neuter gender where text of this agreement so requires. No modification, waiver, termination, recission, discharge, or cancellation of this Agreement shall affect the right of the parties thereafter to enforce any other provision or to exercise any right or remedy in the event of any other default, whether or not similar. This Agreement shall be binding upon and inure to the benefit of the respective parties, their heirs, executors, administrators, legal representatives, successors, and permitted assigns. All provisions of the Agreement shall survive the Closing, and shall not be merged into the delivery of any documents of transfer at the Closing. Each party hereto has had equal opportunity to negotiate the terms hereof, and no provision alleged to be ambiguous shall be construed for or against any party based on the identity of the draftsman of that provision. If any party defaults hereunder, then in addition to other remedies, including specific performance, the defaulting party shall reimburse the non-defaulting party for all of its costs and expenses, including reasonable attorney's fees, incurred in enforcing this Agreement.

IN WITNESS THEREOF, each of the parties has caused this Agreement to be signed, all as of this day and year first written.

SELLER:

BY:_____

BUYER:

BY_____

EXHIBIT SUMMARY

Exhibit A - Specific Assets to be transferred- including furniture and fixtures

Exhibit B - Any liabilities or agreements assumed

Exhibit C - Copy of any leases assumed, or new lease(s)

Exhibit D - Purchase Price explained and sample calculation

Exhibit E - Bill of Sale - allows you to have a document that shows you own the assets without having to show the entire agreement or purchase price.

There is a much more extensive sample asset acquisition agreement provided in the complementary *Acquiring Profit Implementation System*. Below is a sample clause from that agreement, showing how you can add an agreed to allocation of tangible assets vs goodwill.

2.06 <u>Agreement on Allocation of Purchase Price</u>. Buyer and Seller agree that the overall

Purchase Price paid in this transaction shall be allocated as follows:

>the first $_____ to release of the _____ rights as described in Section

1.01 (r) herein;

>the next $_____ to the value of the non-compete agreement described in

Section 9.01 herein: and then

>the remainder of the Purchase Price paid shall be allocated ___% to Goodwill and

___% to non-goodwill Assets listed in Exhibit A (Asset Listing).

In regards to the above allocation of Purchase Price, both Buyer and Seller acknowledge their potential requirements to include IRS Form 8594, "Asset Acquisition Statement." As well as any equivalent state form, in their subsequent income tax filings, agree to coordinate in this regard, and further agree this requirement shall survive until all such filings(s) required by law or regulation are completed and accepted.

Chapter 8: The Closing & Transition

Closing the Deal

At this stage you have, in effect, already launched your partnership with the seller. What is left is the formality of closing the transaction, which means getting the contract signed. But obviously, this can be a very important — and sometimes challenging — formality.

In this chapter, we will present key components to include in the document. We will also discuss some of the important activities surrounding the closing, such as the Kickoff and Merger Announcement, which take place as the acquisition process draws to a dramatic close.

This will be a hectic yet exciting period, with activity swirling around your company. This is not time to lose sight of the details required to complete the transaction and begin the assimilation and integration.

Once the Letter of Intent is signed, you should be moving quickly and methodically towards the contract signing. The timeframe between the LOI and the close depends largely upon the size of the company. With a smaller company, it could be as quick as a couple of weeks or a month — though a larger company might take 45 to 60 days, to order materials and for plan preparation.

The Close

The actual closing should be pretty fast and painless if you have already signed the Definitive Purchase Agreement. The amount of time that has elapsed between the two events will dictate the amount of diligence and verification you typically request.

In an acquisition, unlike a house or building closing, there is no final walk-through. It is important that you make sure there has been no material change in the company since the purchase agreement was signed, such as: significant agent departures, a lawsuit, or other business happenings that change the projected revenue you based the purchase price on. This should be included in the agreement, and have the seller attest to it. If the timespan is more than a week, you will want to review all the updated key performance metrics before closing.

At the time you sign the actual contract, you should also sign a bill of sale (especially in an asset purchase); this document could be necessary if, for example, you are trying to take over management of the website, or even transfer the phone numbers. This document can come in handy as it is a much simpler form to show instead of the entire closing documents, including the purchase price.

At the closing, all pertinent lease agreements and assignment of equipment should also take place. It is also important to get a Blanket Assignment of Contracts, which will include sale contracts, listing agreements, property management contracts, equipment, and office leases. This should cover you if you miss an individual equipment lease not being noted or assigned in the agreement.

Expense Adjustment

We usually request that all the expenses and revenue on the day of closing go to the buyer. Rent and other bills that are monthly or paid annually are prorated so the buyer and seller either receives additional funds or owes them.

Typically, about 30 days later, there will be a "true-up" day. This is when all the bills that were the responsibility of the seller have been paid. If the closing occurs at any other time but the last calendar day of the month, there may be some proration required for some expenses.

An example in the seller's favor is a lease payment that was made in advance for the month, and the credit would be due to the seller for any days when the new buyer accepted responsibility post closing.

An example in the buyer's favor might be a marketing bill that is paid in arrears in which there were expenses earlier in the month that were the responsibility of the seller.

This is a normal practice in an acquisition, and the process and timing should be identified in the DPA.

You Have Acquired A Company! Now What?

After all the closing papers have been signed and the money transferred, the company is yours — congratulations! The real work now begins: to retain the agents, staff, and clients.

It is time to make sure that all the key stakeholders understand what has taken place and are aligned with the vision you will create for the combined entities. Before any news leaks to the general public, or even internally, it is critical to communicate directly with the key people involved on both sides — the agents and staff.

The time to implement your post-closing transition and communications plan has begun. The process of spreading the exciting news may have started a few days before closing, or longer, depending on the need and trust you have in your key people.

"Always remember, although you may have been working on a transaction for months or years and feel like you have hit a goal when you close, it is day one for everyone else," says Mark McLaughlin.

We will typically have a called meeting with our staff late in the afternoon prior to Announcement Day. For the ones who have not been brought in on the process and preparations, we explain the news and what it means for them. We either met with the seller's staff that same afternoon or wait until the next morning for the general agent's announcement.

As we discussed in an earlier chapter, we like to have a reception or dinner the night before the general announcement for the key agents. We allow enough time for the presentation, plenty of questions, and then (hopefully) a happy, pleasant dinner.

Kickoff Or Announcement Day

On the day of the announcement, "impact day," or the "kickoff," you need to have everything well-planned in advance and ready to go. This is the day that, if done well, will create momentum and excitement for the new opportunity for everyone involved.

As the day begins, two separate announcement meetings are usually necessary: You must announce the news within your own company, and you must also announce it to the group that is being acquired.

A lot of the logistics will depend on the size of the groups involved. We have been participants in quite a few well-done and creative announcements.

One company decided to hold the announcement for both companies in the same hotel; the seller's agents' meeting started one-half hour before the buyer's agents' meeting (which should not take as long). This also created some overlap, so the two groups did not run into each other.

For your agents, it is a good idea to have a Q&A handout ready, which provides some background on the company you are acquiring and even some information about individual agents who are joining your team. This will help your agents welcome the new agents and make them feel special. After spending the needed time with the acquired group and answering all their questions, they brought both groups to a new room, decorated with streamers, balloons, refreshments, and live music. They created a true "wow" of a celebration, and it was a great start to the new relationship.

One group we worked with made the announcement in the acquired agents' office and brought a few respected top performers from the buyer's office to share their positive experiences working for the buyer. Afterward, a bus was waiting to take them to a meeting room that was turned into a celebration for both groups.

However you decide to announce, you want to explain the rationale, the benefits, and the individual opportunities. Always remember: What's in it for me?

The seller's agents will want to know how they can transact business today. When do the signs change? What do I say to my clients? Where will my office be? Will my compensation change? You must prepare the answers to any questions they might have in advance.

Announcements done well substantially minimize the risk of agents leaving — or even looking at other options. Your goal for the day is for the acquired agents to leave thinking, "This company really has their act together; they are so professional, and I was greatly impressed that they had thought of everything."

The following is a sample Kick-off/Impact Day Checklist. (You may by now have figured out that we really like checklists.)

Impact Day Checklist - Agents	Date Needed	Date Ordered	Person Resp.	Completed	Comments
1. Location Selected					
2. Catering Menu					
3. Time Confirmed					
4. Agenda Created					
5. Technical/AV Support					
6. Speakers Briefed/Rehearsed					
7. Cards/Badges Wrapped					
8. Prizes Selected					
9. Room Set-up					
10. Decorations					
11. Company Display					
12. New Agent Packets/FAQ					
13. Office Banner Hung					
14. Photographer					
15. Media Notified					
16. Press Releases					
17. Seller Notification Packet					
18. Buyer Notification Packet					
19. Warranty/Referral Offer					
20. Training/Orientation Schedule					

Meeting Your New Team Members

Because the announcements must be made in close proximity time-wise, and it is hard to be in two places at once, regardless of what you have planned, it is a good idea to have some stagger with the timing.

This is important: We have never had luck with allowing the seller to make the announcement alone or without you being there. There are two reasons for this. One is that you have no control over what the seller might say. And the other is that the seller's agents are bound to have immediate questions about how this affects them, and you need to be there for a great first impression by answering all their questions, allaying any anxieties, and selling the benefits and the vision for the combined groups.

The seller should speak to the group first, but please have a mutually agreed-upon script of at least the bullet points of what they will say, which has been rehearsed. This should come from the heart — but also, this is a hugely important event, so practice to make sure all the details are right.

It is a time for the seller to express their gratitude for the agents, explaining that it is their collective hard work that allowed this opportunity to present itself. Hopefully, they can speak to the process of the two firms coming together, the change they were seeking, and how this merger is everything they were looking for to benefit the agents and staff.

The seller should be the one to tell their agents the basic facts of the merger, such as: "We will be closing our office on this date," "We'll be moving to our new location," and what advantages this brings. The seller should also tell them how they fit into the new company and what future plans are.

The emphasis on the seller's presentation should be to convey that they have acted in the best interests of the agents and staff; they should be sending the message: "I truly believe this is the right way to go, please trust me on this; even if you have doubts, give us 90 days to change your mind." Theoretically, the agents at the seller's firm trust the seller and they need to hear this reassuring message before they hear anything from the buyer.

Sharing The Vision

When the seller is finished speaking, they should then introduce you to the group. We like the seller to use both some personal stories and interests of the buyer as well as the business resume, and most importantly, they should share why the seller chose this particular company and person to partner with.

The first thing to do is compliment the seller and his entire company on the outstanding job they have done over the years. Tell them how the seller was determined to find the best fit and greatest opportunity for each of you, and that you are thrilled they chose your company.

Let them know that during this process you have learned quite a bit about the seller and how closely aligned you are, and more importantly, that you have discussed ways to help each of them exceed their goals.

Talk about how excited you are to be bringing together this high-quality professional group with your own strong team that you are equally proud of. Acknowledge that change can be difficult but also exciting and beneficial. Talk about your vision for the new company, the various new tools and programs now available to them, and the opportunities it presents for each of them to accelerate their careers.

Add some "sizzle" to the presentation. You need to make a great first impression, so come up (in advance) with a "wow" for the acquired agents. It may be a few items of the new company's brand on a shirt or jacket, or the outline of a full-page ad with all their pictures coming out in the paper tomorrow or the next home magazine, either in print or digitally.

A few other suggestions we recommend:

- Short presentation on the history of the company and current key metrics.
- Organizational chart and roles of key people (and an introduction if possible).
- An outline of the transition plan, with the dates and times for the upcoming onboarding and training classes.
- Explain what the training will encompass.
- Tell the agents how their sellers will be notified about the changes, anything required of them, and any supporting material that is ready to present, explain, and promote the change.

- Let them know about the media announcements and timing.
- Introduce them to or inform them about the transition team in place.
- Introduce key staff members for your team.
- Alert them to when the new signs will change (ideally, that day).
- Assure them you will do everything you can to minimize any down time during the transition.
- Let them know you are actually expecting listings and business to increase in the next 90 days.
- Hand out individual packages that contain gift-wrapped business cards, a name badge, a car tag (if you use them), and other marketing materials that will be useful.
- Include a handwritten welcome note (if feasible) from the buyer (or manager), which also includes a time and date for a one-on-one counseling session.
- A note to the agent's family is also a great idea, acknowledging their support and all the new tools and teammates their loved one will now have to help them be more successful real estate agents. This is an above-and-beyond idea that people really take notice of.
- Explain in detail the counseling and goal-setting sessions.
- Discuss the alignment of cultures and also the importance of assimilation together.
- Let them know that the seller will still be a critical part of the team and their role, but also how to get in touch with you or their manager.
- We like to have a few respected agents on both sides comment near the end, planned in advance. It is very helpful if a key influencer on the seller's side can, from their chair, say something along the lines of, "We are very appreciative for all the support the seller has provided in the past, and we are excited and looking forward to the new opportunity."

In many cases, we have had good luck getting local dignitaries and press to attend. Placing them near the end of the agenda is best, and you may not want them in the room during the initial announcement. The whole meeting will probably last in the one-to-two-hour range.

After the announcement, if it is a fold-in, visit their new office. Again, it is great when you can create a celebratory atmosphere at their new office and make them feel wanted and welcome.

We have seen many successful events where the party/reception is at the office with the existing agents all ready to greet them and introduce them to the company. It is common, especially in a fold-in acquisition, for the acquired agents to need a little time to process what has happened. Some may be shocked or even angry at the change. Your professional preparation and onboarding will eventually win them over if it does not immediately.

SAMPLE KICK-OFF AGENDA

(Hotel Conference Facility)

8:15-8:30 am	Walk-in Music- Visual Displays/Slides Continental Breakfast
8:30 – 8:40	Seller's Address- The "Why"
8:40 – 9:00	Buyer's Welcome – Vision- Better Together
9:00 – 9:20	New Company – Sizzle- The "What's" in it for me New Agent Value Proposition
9:20 – 9:30	Agent Testimonials- Welcome (Buyer's Company 2-3 respected agents)
9:30 – 9:45	The Next 30 days - Publicity - Training - Seller Notification - "What to do's"/FAQ Handout - New Marketing Material Handout
9:45 – 9:55	Agent Q&A Spontaneous Testimonials (a few planted)
9:55 – 10:00	Joint Seller/Buyer Thank you – next steps

	for the remainder of day and beyond
10:00 – 10:30	Return to Office(s)
10:30 – 11:30	Welcome at Office by Buyer's Agents
	Signage Changed, Materials Ready
11:30 – 1:00 pm	Group/Office Luncheon
1:00 – next 30 days	Individual Key Agent Interviews
	Buyer's Team in Office – Q&A's
	Training/Orientation Sessions Begin

Community Impact

Many acquiring firms try to keep building positive feelings and momentum by scheduling a reception a few days to a couple of weeks after the acquisition for vendors, press, the industry, and the agents' clients (this can be one or separate events). It might be at the office, an event facility, or even a cook-out at the buyer's home.

Another advantage of a Community Impact Day is to bring the agents and staff together to get to know each other better and have some fun. The secondary benefit is to get as much promotional mileage as possible.

You want to make as big a splash as you can afford. At a minimum, you should do a large announcement mailing to clients and the entire real estate community. Ideally, the day of the announcement or on the community impact day, all the signs are changed and the new corporate image is in place everywhere possible.

As you spread news of the new partnership to the outside world, it is very important for all involved to project a positive teamwork image, referring to the union as a dynamic merger of two strong groups rather than an acquisition. The message you want to send to the community is that two great teams have come together and are going to be a major force in the market.

And in reality, that is exactly what is going to happen if you are successful in bringing the two companies and cultures together. That is the final challenge you face, as we will discuss in the next chapter.

SAMPLE ANNOUNCEMENT

ABC Realty, Johnson Realty Merge
Staff Writer, John Doe

Two successful real estate firms in the area have merged forces to create one of the largest independent real estate brokerages in Lake County.

The announcement was made at a breakfast event this morning for both firm's agents and employees at the Westin Lakeview. Those in attendance were told that ABC Realty will be closing their current office and will combine offices as Johnson Realty, at 123 Main Street.

Susan Johnson has operated Johnson Realty for twelve years and she commented on the merger, "We are thrilled to have Jane Jones and her team join us, I have long admired their outstanding professionalism and exceptional service to their clients".

Jane Jones commented, "We are very excited that the merger will allow us to enhance the comprehensive services we will be able to provide to our valued customers and clients. Our agents will now receive the exceptional tools and training provided by Johnson Realty; we could not be happier with the opportunity".

Susan Johnson told the combined audience this morning "in a time of large corporations with hundreds of offices and thousands of agents growing larger, Jane and I felt that combined we could continue to offer a superior service and quality of service unparalleled in the markets we serve, we are committed to being the professional answer to Lake Counties real estate needs.

Jane Jones has owned her company for over 35 years. She has been an award-winning producer and lifetime member of the Platinum Society of the Lake County. She is active in the local Rotary Club having served as a past President. ABC Realty has 11 agents that will be joining the combined firm.

The newly merged office will have over 50 agents, said Ms. Johnson. Johnson Realty has additional offices in Maplewood and Lakewood with a total agent count totaling over 150 including the newly merged Lakeview office. Johnson has been in real estate for 20 years and opened her first office 12 years ago, growing the firm to the largest in Lake County.

Below is a sample checklist of items needed to impact the community. By community, we mean both clients and prospective clients (the market),

Impact Day Checklist - Community	Date Needed	Date Ordered	Person Resp.	Completed	Comments
1. Announcement Date					
2. Sign Need Inventoried					
3. Signs Ordered					
4. Building Banner					
5. Building Signs					
6. Internal Signage					
7. P.R Strategy					
8. Advertising/Marketing Strategy					
9. Sellers Notified					
10. Industry Announcement/Event					
11. Market Area Announcement					
12. Website Announcement					
13. Website Conversion					

Chapter 9: Making It All Work

The contract has been signed. The reception and announcement were huge successes. The two teams have started well, with smiles all around. Does this mean you have got it made?

On the contrary: You have only begun the hard work to ensure the acquisition is a financial win.

The ultimate success of your acquisition will be determined in the months and years after the papers are signed and the welcome speeches have been given. It is in the first few weeks that you will begin to see how well the two sides mesh and whether the acquired agents can fulfill the goals that you established when you first decided to pursue an acquisition.

Horror stories abound about acquisitions that have gone sour during the honeymoon period soon after the closing. Almost every one of those worrisome tales involves one common scenario: agent defections, or the term generally used, breakage.

Without exception, this can turn a potentially successful acquisition into a failure, seemingly overnight. You have lost the thing you spent so much time and effort purchasing. Even if you use our financial risk mitigation strategies, it can still be an emotional and financial blow.

How could such a thing happen? How is it that savvy brokers sometimes get blindsided on the most critical aspect of the entire process? Often it is due to a lack of follow-through on the part of the buyer. Sometimes it is overpromising the acquired agents and under-delivering the end results, or simply not doing what you said you would.

After you have gone through months of the acquisition process, you are probably tired and think it is time to relax — but the reverse is true: You have to be more involved than ever before.

After The Party Ends

Immediately after the acquisition, there is a huge initial surge of excitement and momentum, with a lot of positive talk and many promises being made. The whole atmosphere in the ensuing days, as you celebrate and announce the "merger," is a festive one, and it tends to build great expectations among all the agents and staff — as it should.

But oftentimes, as the party dies down, the buyer gets absorbed in their normal business issues, some they may have been ignoring, and they can become even less visible. The acquired agents don't see anything to back up the talk about the new company and about the new opportunities to increase their business. If this situation goes on for a couple of weeks or maybe months, soon agents begin saying: "This isn't what we were told or expected."

Also know and expect that from day one of the acquisition, your competitors have increased their activity in trying to recruit every agent involved. They are in the agent's ear, telling them it is not going to work out and they have a better opportunity elsewhere. A good transition plan, well-executed, eliminates those issues.

On the other hand, sometimes the problem is not with you, the management team, or even the acquired agents, but rather with your existing ones: So much time and attention has been spent on wooing and welcoming the new people that the existing agents get jealous and start looking around. They feel that you have never spent that much time or attention on them.

It is imperative that you not only be attentive, but also fair-minded; everything that you do for a new agent, such as individual counseling or business planning sessions, you must also do for existing ones. It is important to be positive to all agents but set realistic expectations with what you will offer, promise only those items that you can deliver, and then deliver consistently.

With regard to agent retention, the following is one more Checklist of Considerations to Never Forget.

CHECKLIST OF CONSIDERATIONS TO NEVER FORGET

1. Over-communicate about everything.

2. Rely on your transition team for guidance and feedback.

3. Be available.

4. Work closely with your new agents.

5. Don't forget your "existing" agents.

6. Ask for a little time to prove the benefits.

7. Don't rock the boat — make major changes slowly.

8. Take the best of both companies.

9. Implement great ideas.

10. Take advantage of the momentum.

1. **Over-communicate about everything.** Communicate events, activities, and updates to the entire staff fully and often. To help foster better internal communications and feedback opportunities, you should rely on your "transition team," composed of a few key influencers from each side, to make sure agents and staff are kept well-informed. This could be your existing Advisory Board or President's Club, but it must include some members from the acquired company. Hold consistent meetings for at least the first 90 days. This group will usually spot any issues quicker than you will and can also provide the potential solutions.

2. **Rely On The Transition Team:** You chose the team members based on your trust in them and their influence in the organization. One

of the goals of the transition team is to report back and assist with any issues that may arise. The hope is that the team can catch small issues before they become large ones. This is not "spying" on people; it is just asking them to be aware and assist with any disgruntlement in the course of their normal interactions.

3. **Be Available:** In fact, be *more* visible than you've ever been. People will have a lot of questions, and they are going to need guidance and leadership. Post your available hours, return agent calls and emails quickly, and try to "touch" every agent daily with a check-in minute.

4. **Work Closely With The New Agents:** The people who have been acquired may have a feeling that they have been "taken over." They may be concerned that they will not be treated well at a new company. That is why it is important early to establish a one-to-one rapport with them. Sit down (you or a senior management team member) with every new agent, do goal planning, and get to know them personally.

You do not have to do all of this alone. It is a best practice to pull together your top team players, give them a little money for a lunch outing, and ask them to invite one or two new agents to lunch and help them become part of our team. Some brokerages offer a mentor program to help with onboarding and assimilation. If possible, locate new agent desks near team players and disperse the new agents throughout the office, not all in one section.

5. **Don't Forget Your Exiting Agents:** As you spend time indoctrinating the new agents, the existing ones could feel resentful about not getting as much of your time and attention. Make sure you communicate to them how important they are to you, and try to spend equal time with them.

6. **Ask For A Little Time:** Not everyone is going to be thrilled with the changes taking place, but you should ask everyone, even the obvious naysayers, to at least try to remain neutral for the first 90 days. "We don't want anybody, even non-performers, to leave in the first 90 days," says one broker with a top franchise chain who has acquired many companies. The reason, he says, is because if some people leave — even ones you are fine losing — others may

begin to question what those agents know that others don't. Make a reasonable request of all agents to give it time. Say: "Don't pass judgment until you have given the new company and changes a sufficient amount of time; you won't know if this is the right place for you until you give it your maximum effort to make it work."

7. **Don't Rock The Boat:** Almost any radical change that you make, even if it is an improvement, could be perceived as a negative and give agents a chance to day, "I knew this would happen; the changes are starting." Most brokers try to keep the acquired agents on the same compensation program, or at least give them the option of staying on it.

   Make changes gradually, and remember that it is usually best to implement them after the 90-day mark. This, of course, does not include a material change that may need to be implemented right away, such as the acquired agents moving into your office.

   As with the introduction of any change you will have to state your case as to the reasons for the changes, sell the benefits (hopefully), then demonstrate that the changes are positive, or at least needed.

8. **Take The Best Of Both Companies:** You will probably get the best results if you can find a way to integrate parts of each culture into your "new" company. No matter how successful you have been, there are bound to be things that the acquired company did better than you. The seller and acquired agents will be more supportive of change if you can find something they did well and implement it throughout.

9. **Implement Great Ideas:** After the "dust" has settled, if you were ever going to introduce a new idea, now is a good time to do it. You have more momentum and energy going for you than you've ever had. It is a good time to figure out new solutions to old problems, such as referring leads, what to do with sales meetings, or even your software offerings to agents.

10. **Take Advantage Of Momentum:** With the infusion of new energy and agents, it is a great time for sales contests. For example, you might hold a one-day "telethon" in which agents all come into the office or a conference center and call up past contacts, clients,

and prospects to give them the news about the new merger. Give prizes to agents who make the most contacts, with separate prizes for anyone who sets up a listing or sales appointment, or even a recruiting interview for you. During the day, you can provide lunch and allow some more "bonding time" between the two groups.

Below are many of the items you will want to plan for post closing. Pre-scheduled individual agent follow-up, group activities, orientation program and ongoing training will definitely minimize issues and potential breakage.

Implementation- Post Impact Day	Date Needed	Date Ordered	Person Resp.	Completed	Comments
O 1. 90 Day Activity Calendar					
O 2. Orientation Dates/Program					
O 3. Administrative Training					
O 4. Manager Training					
O 5. Selling Skills Dates					
O 6. Selling Skills Location					
O 7. Value Proposition Training					
O 8. Sales Meeting Schedule/Content					
O 9. Individual Agent Meetings					
O 10. Transition Team Meetings					
O 11. Agent Business Plan Sessions					
O 12. 30/60/90 Day Progress Meeting					
O 13. Weekly Plan Review/Adjustment					
O 14. Seller Input Meetings					
O 15. Career Adjustment Meetings					
O 16. Momentum Recruiting Plan					

When The Honeymoon Is Over

Not every agent will fit your culture — or, more importantly, accept the change. As an example, if you acquire 20 agents, you need to give everyone a chance ... but for how long? It depends. Sometimes you know after just a few days (we hope not); for many, it is a slower process of continued disgruntlement from the agent.

During the first 90 days, you have been meeting regularly with all the new agents and coaching them. At some point you know that the effort, attitude, or acceptance of the changes is not working out for one or more. We recommend another counseling session, laying out the issues and the corrective measures necessary, and even getting advice from the former seller. Because of the earn-out, you want to make sure the seller is aware that you have given the agent every opportunity to fit in, and your conscience should be clear you have given it your best.

If you are confident that it will not work out long-term, then it is time to suggest a career adjustment and cut them loose. It should be positive to both the new agents and your existing ones that you are upholding the company's high standards and you are willing to remove agents who are not going to meet the standards that the other agents (and the company) expect.

If you do get rid of a "bad apple," make sure you let the others know in your one-on-one meetings that you are pleased with *their* efforts and progress. Share with them the positives of what they have been doing, not the negatives of why you had to let someone go. We do not recommend discussing agent firings with others, but sometimes the reasons are necessary for overall morale and the good of the company. Many times, without you even mentioning it, a new agent will say, "our former broker should have gotten rid of them a long time ago."

You also may find that you have an existing agent (one of yours pre-acquisition) or two who have become disruptive or negative due to the changes. They may feel the office is too crowded, or they have serious personality conflicts with a new agent. This may require you to deal with an existing agent because they will not accept the changes and new growth initiative.

This is understandable; not everyone wants to be with an aggressive, growing firm that has renewed expectations. Some would rather be left alone, comfortable with the way it used to be, without any changes or renewed expectations. You might have to point this out after coaching and give them a chance to adapt by saying, "I realize you are not happy here with our recent changes; maybe you should consider moving to a company that isn't as growth- and performance-oriented as we are." (Haven't you always wanted to be able to say this?)

A Great Time To Recruit

As you begin to weed out a few (hopefully not too many) of the non-performers, there will be opportunities to bring in more new people through traditional recruiting efforts.

The post-acquisition time is an outstanding time to recruit. In some ways, you are already in the recruiting mode because you have essentially been recruiting the acquired agents and re-recruiting your existing ones. You are well-practiced in the benefits of your new value proposition. You are also on a roll, with momentum and excitement, so keep it going!

The process of acquiring brokerages that we introduced early-on also applies very well to recruiting agents, from seeking qualified candidates, to making contacts, to the needs analysis and so forth. That same "win-win" philosophy that we have advocated for acquisitions is just as critical to successful recruiting.

Of course, this is also a good time to reach out to other broker-owners in the market to tell them about the transaction, along with your intent to make more acquisitions. You can also use this time to shore up any uncertainty related to pending co-broker transactions that are in the pipeline.

How The Acquisition Checklist Can Also Be Applied To Recruiting

1. Identify quality agent candidates.
2. Establish contact.

3. Build relationship with candidate.
4. Gather information; determine needs and motivation.
5. Determine "potential fit" of agent with your culture.
6. Create and present your value proposition and proposal based on the needs and motivation you have uncovered.
7. Discuss and present "customized" transition and onboarding program.
8. Mutual commitment and agreement.
9. Agent integration and retention through coaching and counseling.
10. Return to step one.

Start Another One

It is now time to reflect and evaluate.

What did you do well in the process of acquiring the firm? In what areas do you feel you need to improve? What will you do differently with the next one?

Few of us really enjoy grading ourselves, but it truly does help to be reflective and assess what you would do differently. Below is a simple "report card" that can be used on a either 1-10 scale or the A, B, C one. You do not have to share this with anyone, but it is important that you evaluate for the next M&A deal.

It can be extremely helpful to ask your key team members to grade the parts of the process they were involved with. You can customize this report card to each team member or even supplement it with individual or team interviews or an evaluation meeting.

It is important to do the assessment while the process is fresh in everyone's minds.

Post Acquisition Self-Evaluation

Report Card

A= Outstanding, B= Good, C = needs improvement

	A	B	C
O Initial Approach/Contact			
O Relationship Building			
O Valuation			
O LOI Presentation			
O DPA/Contract			
O Transition Plan			
O Transition Team			
O Kick-off/Announcement			
O Public Relations Strategy			
O Orientation			
O Integration of Agents			
O 30/60/90 Day Reviews			
O Post closing Recruiting			
O Momentum Created			

Areas to Improve

Generally speaking, once you have successfully completed your first acquisition, you will be much better prepared for the next one.

"It definitely gets easier as you move from one transaction to the next," says Larry Rideout. "With each acquisition, we got better as a team identifying any issues and solving them more quickly — and most importantly, how best to assimilate different personalities into our culture. You will have a lot more confidence with your second acquisition and beyond."

You will undoubtedly learn a lot from your first acquisition. Most take advantage of that hard-earned knowledge and continue to seek acquisition opportunities. Aside from the tangible benefits, such as adding to your bottom line and increasing market share, comes confidence in your management ability that can be sensed by your agents and the marketplace.

After you have done a successful acquisition, even your competitors will take notice. It will let others know what you are capable of and set you apart in terms of the way you are perceived. This will also lead to companies that may be interested in selling contacting you.

Success leads to more success: Agents, and often other owners, want to be part of a growing and dynamic organization.

Buying Home Services Businesses

We do not address buying home services businesses directly in this book. This would include a property management or rental business, construction, maintenance, commercial brokerage, title, insurance, and mortgage firms.

There are some large real estate companies that have all of these divisions or entities, and we have been involved in the acquisition of each type. If the entity you are acquiring has one of these divisions, we strongly recommend getting professional assistance.

The concepts are similar, but each of the home services divisions or entities must be valued separately. These divisions can be combined into one purchase price or offer, but each is uniquely valued.

We still recommend using the adjusted EBITDA approach but the multiples can vary depending on the certainty of income. In most cases, a property management or insurance company will receive a higher market multiple than a normal real estate brokerage firm. The premium is often due to the longer agreements in property management or the quality of repeat customers or "book of business" in an insurance company.

You also want to take into consideration the level of cross-marketing taking place between the entities. As an example, you might only purchase the brokerage firm, and someone else might purchase the mortgage and property management divisions. In this instance, you would have to evaluate the percentage of income that might be lost due to no more clients or leads being sent from those entities.

The bottom line is that the more divisions, the more complex a transaction becomes. This is not to say you should shy away from these entities, as the cross-marketing opportunities can be outstanding — just be careful and seek help.

Addendum A: Case Study — Move-in Acquisition

I. *Needs and Motivation*

> BUYER'S NEEDS AND MOTIVATIONS: Zebra Realty (the buyer) is a 48-agent, 3-office company with sales of $257,000,000. Broker Zelda Zebra and her team have a strong market share position on the west side of their market, but they would like to gain a stronger presence on the east side.

Zelda and her firm are known for their outstanding training programs and agent value proposition. Overall, her needs are:

1. Quickly increase the number of agents without having to undertake a lengthy recruiting process.
2. Increase sales presence and awareness overall in the marketplace.
3. Generate a stronger presence in the east-side market; Zebra currently has several agents working there, and a few listings, but a very small market share.
4. A separate branch office in this market, without undertaking the costs or spending the time necessary to open a new office.
5. Add some management talent.

SELLER'S NEEDS AND MOTIVATIONS: Sun Real Estate (the seller) is a 17-agent, single-office firm with sales of $115,300,000. Broker Susie Sun has seen the company sales level off in the last couple of years, though the company maintains a strong market share on the east side of town, with a good reputation for recruiting quality agents and building strong relationships.

Susie has never considered selling her firm. Susie's needs are:

1. For the company to continue to grow.
2. Develop an ongoing training program to develop her agents.
3. More profit, relieving the stress of the monthly bills.
4. Better overall firm awareness in the market.
5. Continue to grow and develop as a manager and leader

QUESTIONS TO CONSIDER: What is the best approach for Zelda? Would a potential "move-in" acquisition make sense?

Considering Susie Sun's needs, what might the motivations and needs be in considering an offer from Zelda? What kind of role could Susie play in the new larger company?

II. Available facts about Seller

Last Twelve Months (LTM) Financial Statement Shows:

TOTAL Revenues	$ 2,500,000
Commission Expense	$ 1,625,000
Company Dollar/Net Profit	$ 875,000
TOTAL Expenses	$ 800,000
NET INCOME (per statement)	$ 75,000
Adjustments	
Management comp low	$ (20,000)
Fair Market Rent	$ 15,000
Depreciation	$ 10,000
Owner Comm. Split @65%	$ (30,000)
TOTAL Adjustments	$ (25,000)
ADJUSTED EBITDA	**$ 50,000**

We need to make adjustments, as you have previously learned, always.

Susie was paying herself $80,000, but we felt that the market rate and the comp for her going forward would be $100,000, hence the $20,000 deduction from profit. Susie owns the building, but a new lease going forward would be $15,000 less at fair-market value, so we can assume that we can add an extra $15,000 to profit.

Depreciation is a non-cash add-back as part of the formula. Owner personal production is usually an adjustment. In this case, Susie has been leaving 100% of her commissions in the company, so we reduced her profitability by what her commission split would be going forward.

III. Company Valuation:

Based on the available information on Sun Realty, and to keep the numbers simple, we arrived at a market multiple of 4.0 times the adjusted EBITDA of $50,000 for a firm value of $200,000.

This seems like an ideal situation for Zelda Zebra, as Susie is a great recruiter and likes to manage, but she may need additional mentoring on developing agents and agent training, and some relief from actually owning a firm. After adding in a transition budget, Zelda feels she can be aggressive and offer $200,000 for the firm.

IV. The Offer

1. Asset Purchase
2. Estimated Total Purchase Price: $200,000
3. Cash at Closing: $50,000
4. 6% of Company Dollar On Acquired Agents: Three (3) Years
5. 3 Year Lease Plus 2-3 Year Options At Fair-Market Rent.
6. Susie: Branch Manager @$100,000 Total Comp
7. Susie: Allowed Limited Personal Production at 65% split
8. Recruiting Incentive To Be Agreed To For Susie.

We realize that this was a little too perfect and easy for Zelda Zebra, but hopefully you recognize some of the potential issues and areas to consider when formulating an offer.

There should also be some internal synergy savings that Zelda would benefit from, such as absorbing the accounting, purchasing, or marketing into her existing infrastructure.

Addendum B: Case Study — Fold-In Acquisition

I. NEEDS AND MOTIVATIONS

BUYER'S NEEDS AND MOTIVATIONS: James Wilson Realty (the buyer) is a 20-agent, single-office firm with sales of $222 million. Broker James Wilson has a profitable growing operation, but he wants to accomplish the following:

1. Quickly increase the number of agents without having to undertake a lengthy recruiting program.
2. Increase sales and market share.
3. Make better use of the office facility, which has a capacity to accommodate 30+ agents.
4. Maximize the cost efficiency of the current fixed expense infrastructure.
5. Take advantage of Wilson's strong management and administrative support personnel.

SELLER'S NEEDS AND MOTIVATIONS: Hawkins & Co. Real Estate (the seller) is a 12-agent, single-office firm with sales of $100,000,000. Broker Ed Hawkins is the top producer, doing over 40% of the GCI.

Ed has a very good reputation as a sales agent, and his other agents are young with a lot of potential. Hawkins' needs are as follows:

1. A larger company with more visibility to compete in the marketplace.

2. To spend less time assisting agents and more on personal production.
3. To increase profitability of his company.
4. To avoid management duties; Ed does not like managing.
5. Training and developing agents.
6. Determine what to do about the lease on the office, which is expiring in 6 months.

QUESTIONS TO CONSIDER: Does a "fold-in" make sense for Wilson? How about for Ed? Considering Ed Hawkins' personal goals and motivations, what are some of the ways that Wilson might be able to accommodate and help him?

II. Available Facts about Seller

TOTAL Revenues	$ 2,800,000
Commission Expense	$ 2,100,000
Company Dollar/Net Profit	$ 700,000
TOTAL Expenses	$ 450,000
NET INCOME (per statement)	$ 250,000
Adjustments	
Management comp	$ (100,000)
Admin Comp	$ (50,000)
Personal Sales/Auto Expenses	$ 47,000
Interest	$ 15,000
Owner Comm. Split @70%	$ (112,000)
TOTAL Adjustments	$ (200,000)
ADJUSTED EBITDA	**$ 50,000**

We made five adjustments to line items in the financial statements provided.

In this case, the owner, Ed, was taking money out as needed with distributions, which resulted in changes to the management comp and his personal production. There was no management comp being paid, and Ed's spouse was providing legitimate accounting and administrative support for the office with no direct compensation other than through distributions.

This is often the case with producing owners. They will often leave 100% of their commissions in the company and then take out a draw or distribution as needed.

We determined that the company could hire a manager for $100,000 and an administrative support person for $50,000, which resulted in additional expenses and a reduction in profit. Per the formula, we added back the interest that was being paid for a loan that was used to start the business.

Because in a valuation we treat the producing owner as an agent, we adjusted Ed's personal production compensation to what it would be going forward. We also gave him credit as an add-back to profit or his personal auto and car expenses. These expenses were not paid by the company for any other sales associate and would not be going forward.

This financial statement example is created to reflect a real dilemma often incurred by buyers. Ed may believe that he deserves a valuation or purchase price based on a market multiple times the $250,000 shown as net income in the financial statement. It will be the person who does the valuation's job to educate the seller on the true earnings of the company and explain that the management, accounting, marketing, contract support, and so on that he and his spouse provide is a real cost to the business. If these functions are replaced, they will be an expense — or, if they were not performing those functions they could be spending time and effort doing other jobs that would pay them.

The above example shows how important it is for there to be transparency in the valuation process. If there is a wide gap in what each side feels are the true adjusted earnings, it is very difficult to conclude a successful transaction.

III. Company Valuation: Hawkins & CO.

Fortunately, you did a great job of explaining the process and adjustments to Ed. He knows he made a lot of money last year from his personal production, but very little from the company. He even believes he could generate 50% more production if he did not have to run the company at the same time, and he really does not like the hassle of the management side of the business for he and his family.

We have often found that former brokerage firm owners make the best sales associates going forward. They realize how difficult the ownership side is; they have tried it, and know it is not for them.

Based on the available information on Hawkins & Co., and keeping the number simple we suggest offering a purchase price of $200,000 based on a market multiple of 4.0 times the adjusted EBITDA of $50,000. Because this is a potential "fold-in" opportunity, we were a little more aggressive in our incentives. We include the estimated value of those in the offer.

IV. The Offer

1. Asset Purchase
2. Estimated Total Purchase Price: $250,000 (With $50,000 Of Add'l Incentives Included)
3. Cash At Closing: $50,000
4. 5% of Company Dollar On Acquired Agents: Four (4) Years
5. Provide Ed With A Six (6) Month Marketing & Promotion Budget ($25,000)
6. Split The Existing Lease Payments For Up To Six (6) Months ($20,000)
7. Offer To Assist In Marketing The Office Sublease ($5,000)

We added incentives to help make the transaction more appealing to Ed because the synergy opportunities are very large with potential savings in administrative, management, and office occupancy expenses. The incentives are designed to make it easier for Ed to transition into a new company, full-time production, and to get off to a fast start that will benefit you both.

The existing office lease was a big concern to Ed from a stress standpoint. This incentive will help to make his sell decision easier and show your willingness to be a real partner in the transaction.

Again, this was a way-too-easy deal designed to assist in modeling the concepts important to a successful transaction. The ability to add revenue to be supported by your existing infrastructure creates the quickest way to profitability on an acquisition.

We would be remiss without also reminding you that cultural compatibility will be even more important when mixing in a group of new agents into your existing office environment.

Glossary of Terms

ACQUISITION: Technically, it means one company taking over controlling interest in another company. But an acquisition can and should be viewed as a mutually beneficial arrangement in which the seller willingly agrees to give up control of the company to the buyer in exchange for something the seller needs, whether it be cash, future opportunities, or other incentives.

ADJUSTMENTS: Additions or subtractions to the earnings of a real estate company that reflect what a third party would be required to spend based on the revenue and expenses of the company. Adjustments can be accretive to earnings, such as the money spent on a boat that isn't really used in the business, or a family member who is on the payroll for providing service to the business. Or adjustments can deduct from the earnings, such as an owner who does not have a sales manager and is taking no salary for the sales management role they perform.

AGGRESSIVE APPROACH: A conventional short-term win-lose negotiating tactic in which the buyer's primary objective is to acquire a company at the lowest price possible, without consideration for the seller's needs.

ANNUAL COMPANY DOLLAR: The income of a real estate company after collecting gross commissions and fees, then subtracting all commissions paid (sometimes called cost of goods sold).

ANNUAL NET MULTIPLIER: Used as part of the valuation formula, the annual net multiplier is determined by many input variables and can vary by size of firm, market, and economic conditions, to name a few. This is equal to the inverse of the capitalization rate (for example, if the capitalization rate is 25% of one-fourth, the annual net multiplier would be four).

ASSETS & EARNINGS VALUATION: Combines the Net Asset Value Valuation with the Discounted Future Earnings in an attempt to find some mid-range valuation point.

ASSIGNMENT CLAUSE: A clause in an agreement, such as a lease, that specifies how and if that agreement can be assigned to or extended to include another party; this may include notice requirements, financial capacity of the assignee, and the fee required for granting the assignment.

COMMUNITY IMPACT DAY: An event held shortly after an acquisition is completed, usually for the purposes of "introducing" the new, merged company to clients, the real estate industry, the press, and the local community; the event may include a party open to the public, a sign-changing day, and the start of a media campaign.

CONFIDENTIALITY AGREEMENT: Sometimes called a Non-Disclosure Agreement or NDA, this is a written legal agreement between the buyer and seller stipulating that all the non-public information and discussions, and any disclosures, regardless of the outcome of the transaction, must be kept in strict confidence between the two parties and covered representatives.

CULTURE: The overall attitude, approach, and philosophy of a company. The culture is often determined by the owner who attracts agents and staff with a similar attitude and mindset. A company's culture is usually evident in the relationship between agents, as well as in the way the company interacts with the public. Consistent messaging, choosing the right people, and leadership in action is required to maintain the desired culture

DEFERRED PAYMENT: Payment that is made to the seller over an extended period after the acquisition, usually for a predetermined amount and on a certain date.

DEFINITIVE PURCHASE AGREEMENT: A DPA is a legal document that records the terms and conditions between two companies that enter into an agreement for a merger, acquisition, divestiture, joint venture, or some other form of strategic alliance. It is often used in real estate acquisitions and is binding in nature, with the actual closing and money transfer of the business taking place at a later date.

EARN-OUT: Typically, a calculation that is made based on a predetermined percentage of the performance of the agents or company paid by the buyer to seller and agreed to dates. The amount can vary more or less than the estimated purchase price, based on actual results in the year or years following the closing.

EBITDA: Earnings before interest, taxes, depreciation, and amortization. Adjusted EBITDA is the calculation most acquisitions are based on, which reflects the true estimated earnings of the company before tax.

DISCOUNTED FUTURE EARNINGS: Valuation model that suggests the value of the business is better measured by looking at the current and future earnings stream of the business. There are two parts to this process: Determining actual earnings and projecting them in the future, and determining the current value of the future earnings stream to a buyer today.

FIXED COSTS: A cost that remains constant regardless of the sales volume or number of agents; this can include rent on the office space, equipment, administrative support (with excess capacity), and other "overhead" costs.

FOLD-IN: An acquisition in which the buyer closes down the seller's existing operation and then folds the seller's agents (and perhaps staff and management) into the buyer's company.

HIDDEN VARIABLES: Negotiating variables that are not commonly used and which tend to focus on the needs of the seller (i.e., assuming the seller's debt, or providing the seller administrative support, or a marketing allowance).

IMMEDIATE (SHORT-TERM) NEEDS: The needs of the seller that must be addressed right away (usually in 30 days or less), such as debt, tax liens, bills, and so on.

IMPLEMENTATION PLAN: See "Transition Plan"

LETTER OF INTENT: Sometimes called an LOI. A written, usually non-binding proposal to buy a company, presented to the seller. The

LOI specifies what is proposed to be purchased, the price, terms, and typically includes other significant details pertinent to a transaction.

LISTING INVENTORY: All of the property listings that a real estate company and its agents have under agreement; the company's right to sell those properties can be considered as one of the company's valuable transferable assets.

LONG-TERM NEEDS: The seller's long-range goals and aspirations. This can be everything from a desire to retire in X years, to a desire to start a new career or return to personal production. It is the buyer's responsibility to help find the motivation that would inspire a sale and find the solution to help them get there.

MARKET-BASED VALUATION: The market-based business valuation relies upon the comparison of the subject business to similar businesses that have actually sold. There are several sources of market data commonly used, including publicly traded company purchases and sales, private company sales, and any previous sales of the subject business.

MERGER: A combination of two companies through a pooling of interests. The primary difference from an acquisition is that in a merger, the seller usually maintains some level of shared ownership in the new company. Note that in the M&A world, when the term "merger" is used, it is probably an acquisition with the seller retaining no ownership in the buyer's company.

MOVE-IN: An acquisition in which the buyer assumes the existing operation of the seller, including the facility. Typically, the seller's offices, agents, and staff are kept in place. The buyer moves in (ownership) and changes the signs and brand (and may or may not install new management, agents, and/or policies).

NEEDS ANALYSIS: The process, formal or not, in which the buyer attempts to consider and analyze the needs and motivations of the buyer. The seller is trying to find a problem or opportunity to solve.

NEGOTIATING VARIABLES: Commonly used bargaining chips that can be offered to a seller and used to raise or lower the price accordingly.

(For example: paying cash at closing, paying a percentage of the pending sales as they close, or paying based on the performance of the agents, to name a handful.)

NET ASSET VALUATION: The net asset approach bases the valuation upon the size of the asset base that has been created as a result of past operations. In simplest terms, it represents the liquidation value of the firm. In most instances, this approach will produce the lowest estimate of the firm's value, particularly for the firm that continually operates at a profit.

OWNER COMPENSATION: The various means by which a broker/owner is paid or otherwise rewarded by their own company; this can take the form of salary, percentage of sales, commission draw, or other private company perks, such as a car, boat, or "business" vacations.

PENDING (PENDING SALE): The buyer and seller of a real estate property have agreed to the price and terms, and signed a binding agreement to close on the property at a future designated date.

P&L STATEMENT: Profit and loss statement, also referred to as a financial statement or an income/expense statement, which shows company revenues and expenses on a monthly and/or annual basis. This is an unaudited "internal use" statement, with the categorization of income and expenses (and the recognition of such) varying widely.

PRO FORMA: The best estimate of what a company's revenues and expenses will be for a given time period in the future.

POTENTIAL FIT: An attempt to judge, in advance, whether two companies are compatible and how they would blend together in an acquisition. Compatibility is determined through a comprehensive review of the business model, offering, policy and procedures, operations, and culture during the process.

RELATIONSHIP BUILDING: The development of a rapport between the buyer and seller based on mutual trust and respect. It begins with the first contact.

RISK SHARING: Structuring the terms of the acquisition that maximizes the seller's financial potential and reduces the risk to the seller of under-performance after the acquisition closes. This strategy allows the seller's total payout to increase as the risk is shared based on actual future results.

SAVING FACE: Helping the seller to maintain a sense of pride and accomplishment even as they are selling the company, as well as after the company is sold. This can be accomplished with a title, a new role in the company, or simply by treating the seller with respect in all interactions with agents and the community.

SELLING THE VISION: Convincing the seller you have a strong and workable plan to unite the two companies and that you are the person to lead it. This takes place through the entire process, proving by your actions that you are worthy to lead the firm the seller has built (and their agents) into the future.

SPLITS: Referring to the commission agreement between the company and the agent, or the percentage of commission that is paid to the agent on a sale.

TARGET LIST: A list of companies that would be considered suitable acquisition candidates; a buyer usually ends up with a number of companies that would be their preferred candidates, which are often called "targets."

TRANSITION PLAN: Developed by the buyer and their team before the actual purchase of the company and refined after the LOI is signed. The plan maps out all the activities, the person responsible, dates, and steps necessary at the time of closing and immediately after to ensure a successful integration and assimilation of the acquired agents. This is also sometimes referred to as the "implementation plan."

TRANSITION TEAM: A core group of key members of both companies assembled prior to closing, whose responsibility is to provide guidance, feedback and do the work required for a successful integration.

UNDERLYING NEEDS: The needs of the seller that may be hidden or not openly discussed: these can include recent agent or staff defections, personal problems, office conflicts, and more.

UPFRONT PAYMENT: Payment (usually cash) that is made to the seller at the time of closing or shortly after.

VALUATION FORMULA: Any number of existing established formulas that can help a buyer determine how much a company is worth and how much they can pay; such formulas usually provide a rough estimate or value range, as opposed to a precise number. Terms are as important as price.

VALUE PROPOSITION: Services, tools, and facilities that are provided by the broker that assist the agents and help them to be productive, which might include training programs, the brand, marketing programs, technology stack, and administrative support.

WIN-WIN APPROACH: A philosophy toward business dealings, and in particular, negotiations between two companies, which stresses that both parties must benefit and be satisfied if a deal is to be successful ultimately. This runs counter to traditional approaches, which tend to view negotiations as a win-or-lose situation, in which side always comes out better.

Concluding Thoughts

If you are reading this page, you have made it through the complete life-cycle of an acquisition of a real estate brokerage firm. Congratulations, and thank you for wading through a sometimes dry and difficult subject!

If you are contemplating your first transaction, we are hopeful that you now have enough confidence to begin or continue the process with a potential prospect. If you have already completed your first acquisition or are an "old pro" at it, we hope you were able to pick up a pointer or two that will make your next one a little easier.

We wanted to present in as fair a picture as possible the process, time, and effort required to perform a successful acquisition. We in no way meant to scare you or warn you away from embarking on an exciting way to grow your company. We believe as many top real estate firms in the U.S. have proven that M&A, done well, is the quickest and most profitable way to grow your company.

Our best advice to you, even after all the knowledge you have gained in this book, is to ask for help. There are many very experienced firm owners that can share helpful tips; there are industry resources available; there are firms that specialize in M&A advisory. WAV Group and our M&A Advisory Division is, based on results, the preeminent M&A Advisory team in the industry. We can assist in any and all phases of the entire M&A process, from strategic planning, market research and prospecting, to valuations, negotiations, and public relations.

Our initial consultations are always free. You can reach us on our website at www.wavgroup.com or order the Acquiring Profit Implementation System directly at www.wavgroup.com/amp

It would be our pleasure to assist you.

Acknowledgments

We would sincerely like to thank all who have contributed to this book. We realize that we will leave so many important people out who have contributed to our experiences and knowledge used in this book; for that we are sorry. Please also accept that any mistakes in this book are ours alone.

We especially want to acknowledge the following people for their direct assistance with our book endeavor;

Monika Sollee assisted us in every phase of the process, Jason Parker who helped with the digital and print versions, Amber Taufen did amazing work editing our text and making it readable, Gordon Wong created our graphs and charts, and Mark Gelotte for the cover.

Many thanks to our colleague's Mark McLaughlin, and Finley Hair for their support, contributions and insight. We are also grateful to those that provided stories, anecdotes, and offered improvements including Larry Rideout, Paul McGann, Howard "Hoby" Hanna IV, John Fetherston, Lacey Merrick Conway, Gino Blefari, Pat Shea, Anthony Lamacchia, and RJ Long

For all those mentioned above and those we failed to mention your assistance was invaluable and much appreciated. Your contributions have made the finished product so much better.

About the Authors

George Slusser

George Slusser is a true industry pioneer and visionary. Over the course of his career, he has been an active participant in 1,000+ M&A transactions with a collective purchase price more than $1.5 billion. He helped define and advance the Real Estate Brokerage M&A industry with his groundbreaking and best-selling book, *Acquiring Profit*. He was the first to recognize, practice, and teach that there was a repeatable process in every successful transaction. George emphasized in his work that the financial remuneration and terms, although important, were not necessarily accurate indicators of success. He stressed the critical importance of cultural compatibility and allowing a win/win outcome for both sides of the transaction.

George entered the real estate industry following the receipt of his M.B.A. Degree. He was taught well and mentored in M&A by the numbers at Merrill Lynch. During his tenure, he co-created the acquisition process, system, and tools used throughout the Merrill Lynch Realty brand.

George took his "Wall Steet" experience with Merrill Lynch to many senior executive roles in the real estate industry. His unique experience and skill set allowed George to be highly sought after. He has been involved in many of the major M&A initiatives that have helped shape the industry. He assisted in Coldwell Banker Corporation's and ERA Real Estate Corporation's purchase and assimilation by CENDANT, now named Anywhere. He was tapped to assist with GMAC's acquisition of the Better Homes & Gardens brand. George was a major contributor, helping NRT become the world's largest brokerage firm through leading the large brokerage acquisition strategy.

George also served as Global President of Coldwell Banker Commercial Real Estate. There he enabled record-breaking growth for more than 500 branded brokerages and more than 7,500 agents worldwide. Following CBC, George is credited with helping more than triple royalty revenue as Chief Operating Officer and Chief Growth Officer at SVN International, the world's largest commercial real estate franchise organization. There he led M&A activity and franchise sales with expansion into 6 countries.

Following his stint at SVN, George joined WAV Group as a Partner in 2021 to launch and lead the M&A Advisory Services Division. There he utilizes a proven team of industry veterans who provide a wide array of Advisory Services including; strategic planning, succession planning, valuations, research, and buy or sell side representation. They help clients both large and small, with anything ranging from partnership changes or small mergers, to the largest and most complex transactions in the industry.

You can find out more about their services by visiting www.wavgroup.com or email George for a complimentary consultation at george@wavgroup.com.

Victor Lund

Victor Lund brings a wealth of business experience and is a founding partner of WAV Group. Lund's MLS consulting focuses on operational effectiveness and strategic planning. Brokers and franchises work with Lund on technology selection, optimization and adoption. Technology companies engage Lund for market development, problem resolution, and product positioning strategies.

Victor is known for leveraging a vast industry perspective, helping clients see first what others see eventually.

In addition to his consulting role with WAV Group, Lund is a founder and CEO of RE Technology, the leading real estate technology and media portal in the United States with more than 1 million visits a month.

Victor founded WAV Group with his partners in May 2004. Previously, Lund and partner Marilyn Wilson operated Wilson Victor Associates.

This business-consulting firm served their clients in the areas of new business development and new product development before being joined by Michael Audet.

In addition to his activities as a consultant, Mr. Lund was also an associate with the venture capital firm Resource Capitalist, LLC from 2000 to 2004. Lund led the business plan review team, working closely with entrepreneurs and technology start-ups in developing and funding their businesses. Today Lund focuses venture activities on private placement.

Mr. Lund was raised in family controlled businesses, Lund American and Dynamic Homes. Lund American, the world's premier aluminum boat manufacturer.

Inman News selected Victor Lund as one of the Top 100 Influential Leaders in the Real Estate Industry. He has also been selected on The T360/Swanepoel Power 200 and RISMedia Newsmaker 200.

Victor can be reached at victor@wavgroup.com.

Printed in the USA
CPSIA information can be obtained
at www.ICGtesting.com
JSHW010314280823
47207JS00001B/2